◆ HOW TO ROCK CLIMB SERIES ◆

More
Climbing
Anchors

15370

◆ HOW TO ROCK CLIMB SERIES ◆

More Climbing Anchors

John Long

Bob Gaines

FALCON®

Guilford, Connecticut
An imprint of The Globe Pequot Press

◆ HOW TO ROCK CLIMB SERIES ◆

How to Rock Climb!
by John Long

Sport & Face Climbing
by John Long

Big Walls!
by John Long and John Middendorf

Knots for Climbers
by Craig Luebben

Climbing Anchors
by John Long

Flash Training
by Eric Hörst

Gym Climb!
by John Long

Build Your Own Indoor Climbing Wall
by Ramsay Thomas

Nutrition for Climbers
by Beth Bennett

Clip n' Go!
by John Long and Duane Raleigh

**The I Hate to Train
Performance Guide for Rock Climbers**
by Nancy Prichard

Self-Rescue
by David Fasulo

ISBN 0-57540-000-6

Manufactured in the United States of America
First Edition/Second Printing

WARNING: CLIMBING IS A SPORT WHERE YOU MAY BE SERIOUSLY INJURED OR DIE.

READ THIS BEFORE YOU USE THIS BOOK.

This is an instruction book to rock climbing, a sport which is inherently dangerous. You should not depend solely on information gleaned from this book for your personal safety. Your climbing safety depends on your own judgment based on competent instruction, experience, and a realistic assessment of your climbing ability.

There is no substitute for personal instruction in rock climbing and climbing instruction is widely available. You should engage an instructor or guide to learn climbing safety techniques. If you misinterpret a concept expressed in this book, you may be killed or seriously injured as a result of the misunderstanding. Therefore, the information provided in this book should be used only to supplement competent personal instruction from a climbing instructor or guide. Even after you are proficient in climbing safely, occasional use of a climbing guide is a safe way to raise your climbing standard and learn advanced techniques.

There are no warranties, either expressed or implied, that this instruction book contains accurate and reliable information. There are no warranties as to fitness for a particular purpose or that this book is merchantable. Your use of this book indicates your assumption of the risk of death or serious injury as a result of climbing's risks and is an acknowledgment of your own sole responsibility for your climbing safety.

To my wife, Mariana Rondon-Mendez.

About the Authors

John Long, a veteran of fabled Camp 4 in the Yosemite Valley, has been climbing, adventuring and writing for much of his life. In addition to pioneering the *How To Rock Climb!* series, he also has several works of adventure fiction to his credit, including *Gorilla Monsoon* and *Rock Junction,* compliations of short adventure fiction.

When he's not on the rocks or in front of the computer writing, he's in Venezuela with his wife and two daughters.

Bob Gaines is an American Mountain Guides Assocation Certified Rock Climbing Guide and director of Vertical Adventures, and AMGA accredited rock climbing school in Newport Beach, California.

C O N T E N T S

MORE CLIMBING ANCHORS

JOHN LONG
BOB GAINES

*Colin Lantz on TGV,
(5.13c), Industrial Wall,
Colorado.*

Beth Wald photo

Climbing on The Shield, El Capitan, Yosemite, California.

Beth Wald photo

Introduction

Climbing gyms, training programs, bouldering, the benign character of many bolted sport routes, plus the sport climbing revolution's drive toward high numbers have resulted in climbers tackling extreme routes with far less experience than in years past. In as little as six months, some rookies are already leading 5.10, even 5.11 routes. But what kind of 5.11 routes? The question is crucial.

Control is the game with bolted sport routes. Run outs are scarce. Injuries are rarely the result of a fall, but most commonly the effect of pulling too hard (muscle and tendon tweaks). The end result is that today's sport climbing milieu has sometimes fostered attitudes and expectations that spell trouble—namely, that a climber schooled exclusively on bolt protected sport routes is ready to go, say, to Yosemite or the Italian Dolomites and tackle big, legendary adventure climbs. Judging by his or her success on the sport climbs, at least in terms of the numbers (for instance, she may routinely lead 5.12 at a sport crag), isn't it a sure bet that she'll cruise a 5.10 "trad" route first climbed thirty-five years ago, before chalk, sticky boots, belay devices, Spandex, even before tattoos and nose rings? Absolutely not. The only sure bet is that if she is not fluent in placing her own protection and running the rope out above it—sometimes a perilously long way—and does not understand the rudiments of arranging sound belays, that twenty pitch, minimal 5.10 route might seem like a junket to hell. Many young sport climbers are discovering just that. The hard way.

A false notion coming from the sport climbing world is that genuine cranking is something new. A tour of old bouldering gardens will confirm that, though standards have steadily risen, folks have been pulling down for going on forty years. The practice was not exercised on roped climbs because to do so required a profusion of bolts considered unacceptable till this last fifteen years. Hence, the traditional testpieces were much more a trial of leading prowess—often requiring craft in placing protection and anchors—than in executing ghastly moves. The climbers of old had the advantage of following the standard program of working up through the grades, step by step, learning the subtleties of placing gear and making mistakes on routes that were forgiving enough not to cost them dearly. The modern day climber follows a more accelerated agenda. Peer pressure and tradition insists that you jump straight onto bleak terrain, and the bombproof fixed protection and anchors on most sport climbs means that anyone with rock shoes and a chalk bag can usually do so and pay little or nothing no matter how miserably you fail. Not the case on the old trad routes. And here lies the problem. Climbers trained exclusively on sport routes often lack the experience to adequately safeguard their forays onto trad routes. They simply haven't placed enough nuts and rigged sufficient anchors to know what is good and what is disastrous. This goes far in explaining the glut of accidents occurring on the old classics. Annual accident reports tell us inexperience and poor judgment are normally the cause for misadventures. A second factor is that many modern climbers are one-dimensional: they might float up a horrid, overhanging face climb, but thrash like a gaffed tarpon on a chimney or a greasy offwidth crack.

This begs the obvious question: If you are a sport climber—and odds say that you are—why concern yourself with learning elaborate rigging techniques if it's only the bolted short routes that interest you? The answer: if you stick with climbing long enough, your taste will invariably change. You might never stray far from sport routes, but that first generation of kids who broke in on bolted face routes and in climbing gyms have now been around for a decade or more, and he or she is the rare climber who has not on occasion gone adventure climbing. It's natural to do so. If you have years invested in the sport you'll likely not hang up your boots before making a lap up El Capitan or the Diamond, or at least taking a crack at some of the celebrated, long free routes in Zion, Red Rocks, Yosemite, or wherever. And said routes require that you place protection and rig often complex anchors, skills rarely needed on modern sport climbs. For these reasons, the art of placing protection and arranging belays is a vital concern for today's climbers, and is part of the reason behind this second volume on anchors.

The purpose of this manual is to expand on the material covered in the first volume (*Climbing Anchors*), and to introduce a few current, little-used rigging techniques. *More Climbing Anchors* does assume you have a working understanding of the systems presented in the first book. However, several crucial issues are worth reviewing.

First is that we strive to build anchors that are Solid, Redundant, Equalized and that allow No Extension, or SRENE. (This acronym is modified from one used by the American Mountain Guides Association.) The fundamental concepts behind SRENE are:

SOLID means the individual anchors and the system as a whole must be bombproof, able to stop a rogue elephant, without question.

REDUNDANCY generally means placing three or four solid anchors (more if the anchors are less than ideal). Never use only one nut. Never. Most experienced climbers don't consider an anchor secure until they have set a minimum of three good nuts. Two bombproof anchors is the absolute minimum. In emergencies, climbers occasionally will use a single bolt, tree, or tied-off boulder for an anchor, but secure backup anchors will greatly reduce the chance of catastrophe. Redundancy should exist through the entire anchor system: all anchors, slings and carabiners should be backed up. Redundancy also can include setting anchors in more than one crack system, to avoid relying on a single rock feature.

EQUALIZATION distributes the load equally between the various anchors in the system, to increase the overall strength of the system and to reduce the chance of a single anchor pulling out, no matter the cause (shockloading, etc.).

NO EXTENSION means that if one of the anchors or components in the system should fail, the system will not suddenly become slack and drop the climber a short distance, shockloading the remaining anchors.

Though we will not always be able to construct anchors that conform perfectly to SRENE standards, that is our goal.

Establishing complex anchors is chiefly a matter of rigging, knowing how best to connect the various components of the anchor matrix. This requires both engineering and improvisation.

Rigging slings and equalization systems are largely technical skills, but setting nuts, SLCDs (spring-loaded camming devices), then keeping the whole works clean and simple is very much an art. Understand this: Excepting some bolt anchors, every anchor varies in detail, and there is rarely a "best" method per the details. Put a dozen certified guides in a bar and bring up the topic of belay anchors, and you'll hear a dozen different opinions about the "right" way to handle the fine points. And for the most part, they'll all be right. But fine points are a different matter than basics, and per the basics, every able guide is in agreement: A sound anchor is Solid, Redundant, Equalized, and allows No Extension when shockloaded (SRENE).

While there is often no "best" way to rig an anchor, there are countless wrong ways, or at least methods that are inferior to others. This book has attempted to point out both viable rigging methods and ones that are suspect. Concerning the viable methods, when the anchor is complex, where there are four or five nuts, several slings, cordelettes, tricky equalizing constructs, et al. (as featured in many of the examples herein), it is futile to memorize the given system and to try and replicate it in the field. The point is to study the factors and rigging involved and to grasp how certain standardized methods are properly used. The anchors you will construct on the rock or in the mountains must take specific factors into account (such as placements, location, and so forth), and the specifics are far too varied to encapsulate in a short book. Most every anchor presents challenges that must be solved on the spot. Providing you understand the basic, standardized principals and a handful of rules of thumb, and know them well enough to improvise on the theme as circumstances demand, a sound anchor is usually available for you. So again, it's not so much the minutia of the examples in this text, as the broad principles, that you should study and make your own.

The science and art of setting anchors evolves with new equipment and new knowledge, and the whole study is open ended. Every book has limitations, and our limitations are mainly a matter of space. This book is not a stand-alone anchor manual. That would require at least 500 pages. Much has been left out that is important, but we've tried to concentrate on those scenarios that today's climber will most likely face. As other relevant information and photos come in, we'll round it up into another book. For now, we trust that what follows will further safety in a potentially perilous sport. For as legendary Canadian wall climber Hugh Burton once commented to me, "Without a good anchor, you've got nothing."

RULES OF THUMB

The following pages show photographs of specific anchoring systems, along with an evaluation on the features involved. These evaluations deal primarily with specific factors; the following "Rules of Thumb" set down general considerations, and are a reference point that, when appropriate, will be noted in the evaluation (e.g. Ref. Rule of Thumb #3.). Reference to a rule of thumb invites you to refer back to this section and review the rule—and to keep reviewing the rule till it's burned into memory.

Cordelette Usage

In the three brief years since *Climbing Anchors* was first published, the cordelette has caught on as an invaluable tool with many applications. The principal merits of the cordelette are expressed by the acronym SEB: "S" for Simple, in terms of the simplest system using the least gear and minimum engineering stunts; "E" for Easy, referring to the ease and speed you can construct and clean a given anchor; and most importantly, "B" for Bombproof, which is self-explanatory. Again, the "S" in SEB means anyone in-the-know can quickly rig a multi-component anchor, and quickly. The E in SEB means you can forgo all of those confounding and time-consuming Quickdraw/sling/biner constructs trying to equalize those four nuts. Just hitch the whole business together with a cordelette (illustrated in detail later on), ponytail the ends together, tie them off with a figure eight and you have a B for Bombproof. Lastly, the cordelette does not eat up lead rope. Few routes require the entire 165 feet of line, but if one does, and you've got a dozen feet of lead rope spiderwebbed in the belay anchor, what will you do when you're hanging off bleak crimpers and have run out of rope a dozen feet shy of the bolts? Curse yourself for not bringing a cordelette....

The limitation of the cordelette is that it always results in a mono(one)-directional anchor. That is, force is distributed equally to various components of the anchor only when the cordelette is loaded in one direction, usually straight down. In technical argot, cordelette use depends on the vectoral impacts (forces) it is required to withstand, and the relative stability and directional analysis of it's components.

Rule of Thumb #1A: Avoid using the cordelette when you require a multi-directional, equalized anchor.

Rule of Thumb #1B: A piece(s) in opposition with the cordelette's one good direction is very helpful and good practice. Oblique angles on the anchor will always affect the piece(s), and a larger angle will give a greater load.

Sliding knot

Rule of Thumb #2A: Appropriate use is related to the anticipated direction of loading.

Rule of Thumb #2B: The sliding knot is the best, true equalizing method.

Rule of Thumb #2C: There is no redundancy with one sling.

Rule of Thumb #2D: There are always trade offs with using the sliding knot: A) good equalization versus extension—meaning the sliding knot achieves almost perfect equalization between two or more placements, but if one placement blows, the sling will extend and shock load onto the other piece(s); and B) multi-directionality versus component security—meaning the sliding knot can be pulled in various directions and will adjust accordingly, however, the sliding knot does not always keep direct pressure on the placements unless the anchor point itself is weighted. And with marginal placements, whose security depends on said placements not moving or shifting, it might sometimes be better to lash the placements in snug opposition to other placements (using, say clove hitches on a sling).

Rule of Thumb #2E: If the direction of loading is uncertain, the sliding knot is the first choice. If the direction of loading is known, it may be better to use a cordelette or slings in an individual component equalizing system.

Rule of Thumb #2F: If the components are poor, it is crucial to minimize extension potentials.

Horizontal, non-fixed anchors

The text shows various examples of horizontal anchors, most of which, if not ideal, are at least cooperative. Often the protection components are not available for the directions desired.

Rule of Thumb #3A: Sometimes it is required to rig horizontal placements with a system using large angles, and to perform other tricks to compensate for increased loads.

Rule of Thumb #3B: Direction and multi-directional equalization are crucial here, especially on traversing routes.

Rule of Thumb #3C: Force systems are complicated, so place more pieces rather than less, and be careful.

Load on the climbing rope

Rule of Thumb #4A: The climbing rope should always run through the equalized anchor point.

Climbing rope used to rig the anchor's components

It is a great last resort—and a viable first resort given perfect and predictable conditions. However it is often a poor technique for longer routes, and is no longer considered a standard method.

Rule of Thumb #5A: Yields laborious and dubious equalization.

Rule of Thumb #5B: Harder and more confining to change over.

Rule of Thumb #5C: Harder to escape from and retreat in case of emergency.

Rule of Thumb #5D: Uses more rope, sometimes needed for the following lead.

Rule of Thumb #5E: Harder to rig an equalized directional.

Upward-oriented directional below the equalized anchor point

Rule of Thumb #6A: Defines the direction of the components' loading.

Rule of Thumb #6B: Adds anchor security

Rule of Thumb #6C: Crucial for belaying the leader above, where upward forces are a real possibility.

Evaluating an anchor—crucial factors

Rule of Thumb #7A: The security of the components.

Rule of Thumb #7B: Position.

Rule of Thumb #7C: Intended use.

Rule of Thumb #7D: Anticipated direction of loading.

Rigging (Redundancy, Equalization and No Extension, in that order)

A note on strategy for teaching anchoring techniques:

Stress overkill (and even over-rigging) because few beginners can distinguish a good placement from an atrocious one. Overstressing that an ornate system is inferior to a simpler one is a philosophy that only applies to experts—though if an anchor is too cluttered and complicated to evaluate and understand, that too can be dangerous.

Luke Laeser in the Rappel Gully, Shiprock, NM. Photo: Cameron Burns

Bruce Anderson belaying on
The Nose, *El Capitan*
Photo: Cameron Burns

Multi-bolt Sling Belays

Bigger, stronger bolts mean that today's typical sling belay is capable of absorbing higher forces than sling belays of a dozen years ago. Before the sport climbing revolution, the standard bolt was the ¼" Rawl contraction bolt, a tool principally designed to provide temporary anchorage in masonry and cement, not to safeguard against leader falls or to secure a permanent belay anchor. Time has shown that these ¼" bolts eventually work loose, and are prone to corrosion and work hardening. Many have failed, and consequently they are no longer used or trusted.

The five-piece Rawl has become the bolt of choice. Given that the bolt is set in quality rock, even the shortest (⅜"-by-2") of these carbon steel bolts has a sheer strength of 7,825 lbs. Both computer analysis and lab tests indicate that, given the dynamic properties of the modern climbing rope, it is almost impossible for a 165 lb. climber to generate more than 2,100 lbs. of force on an anchor, no matter how long a fall he or she might take.

Because two, sometimes three bolts are featured at most modern sling belays, there is so much overkill built into the system that a multi-bolt belay, properly engineered and rigged, is strong enough to hang your car off. Poor rock can compromise the strength of the anchor, but that's the risk everyone takes who climbs on junk rock.

Yes, the typical sling belay has benefited from both new equipment (namely, the bigger, stronger bolts and hangers) and improved rigging techniques. And yet twenty years ago, in the age of ¼" Rawl bolts, when most climbers never equalized the anchor but simply clipped in with overhand knots, and when everyone belayed with the rope running round their hips, total belay failure was exceptionally rare.

This is all the more remarkable considering that the adventure climbs of twenty years ago, while technically easier than today's gymnastic sport climbs, often featured longish runouts with abundant chances for huge falls (which many climbers took). Still, the fact that the old rigging methods were good enough in all but exceptional circumstances does not stop us from searching out newer, safer methods.

To my knowledge I have never heard of the total failure of a correctly arranged, multi-bolt sling belay featuring the five-piece Rawl bolts (given that they are set in good rock).

Where the elaborate equalizing systems come into their own is when the sling belay on an old adventure climb has not been removed and replaced, but simply shored up with one new bolt. Here you are left to deal with several corroded bolts and the new one, and this is when the new rigging techniques really shine.

Also discussed is the "Atomic Clip," a clean and efficient method of anchoring off to a two-bolt sling belay. The Atomic Clip is rarely seen, but is not new, nor is it significantly better than other methods. However it is a tool that has advantages, and is worthy of addition to our bag of rigging tricks. Since it requires using a knot common only to rescue work—the bowline-on-a-bight—time will tell if the Atomic Clip will catch on.

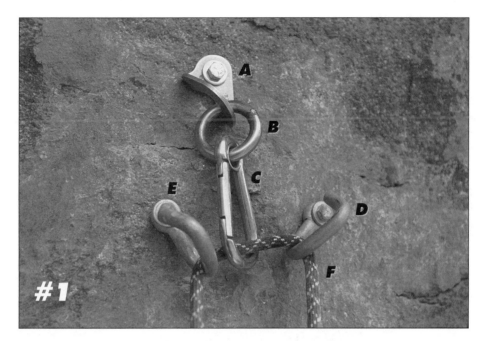

ANCHOR #1: Two open cold shuts (D, E) backed up with a new, stainless steel "Fixe Sport Anchor" consisting of a five-piece Rawl stud and stainless steel hanger (A), a welded stainless ring (B) connected to a permanent stainless biner (C).

PRO: This is a well-engineered, extremely strong setup.

CON: Cold shuts should be made of stainless steel, not soft steel, iron, or aluminum, all of which wear rapidly when a doubled rope is pulled through the anchor, or when the climber is lowered; in both instances the running rope grooves the shut. These shuts should be replaced with the new stainless steel article if the route sees much traffic.

COMMENTARY: Two open cold shuts (the standard setup on most sport climbs) should only be used for lowering/toproping, never for anchoring a hanging belay. This setup is normally found at the "end" of a short sport climb, where upon gaining the belay, the leader can simply loop the rope through the open shuts, clip through the Fixe anchor for a backup, and lower to the deck, everyone else toproping through the system. However, when the pitch is so long that a doubled rope is too short for the leader to lower all the way back to the deck, he or she must either pull up and attach another rope, or belay off the Fixe rig. If so, never clip biners straight into the open shuts, rather hitch the shuts off with slings, and back this up by clipping a proper, locking biner through the stainless steel ring on the Fixe rig.

As always, never blindly trust/use any system, even this one. Always ask questions: For instance, are all three bolts in a big loose block? Is the anchor in a good position?

#2

ANCHOR #2: Two bolts (A and B), four hardware store variety Quicklinks (C and D), and a rope (E) rigged for a rappel.

COMMENTARY: This setup is becoming increasingly popular at many sport climbing areas. The Quicklinks are wrenched down tight, and become a fixed biner through the bolts, thus eliminating the mess and confusion of a wad of fixed slings and dicey old rappel rings. Two things to make certain of: 1) if you are belaying/lowering/rappelling directly off Quicklinks or chain links, the narrower angle the links form (meaning the closer the bolts are together), the less force is placed on the bolts. If the bolts are, say, eighteen inches apart, when you weight the anchor the downward force pulls the links toward each other and the strain put on the bolts is dramatically higher—this issue will be taken up in greater detail later on—2) As is the case with any fixed anchor, eyeball the links. The newer links are stainless steel and stronger than God. They are also expensive, so it's not unheard of that a man would endeavor to fleece the communal links, by main force if necessary, including hammering the threaded sleeve to loosen it. So inspect all Quicklinks or chain links before trusting them outright.

Photo: Beth Wald.

BOWLINE-ON-A-BIGHT

Use and applications:

The bowline-on-a-bight has been around since Noah's Ark, has long been a favorite in rescue work, but only recently has it been espoused as a viable knot for sport climbing. As seen in forthcoming examples, the bowline-on-a-bight can be rigged to function much the same as a cordelette, the difference being that the bowline-on-a-bight has only two branches. It's particularly useful in equalizing two bolts at a hanging belay. Fast to arrange, it uses the climbing rope as rigging, eliminating extra slings and Quickdraws normally required to equalize an anchor (it also swallows up footage off the lead rope). And as we will see, the bowline-on-a-bight is also handy to equalize two points of a multi-component anchor. Be aware, however, that whenever you use the rope to equalize the anchor, in the event of an emergency you'll have to rerig in order to escape. This takes time and effort.

Much like the clove hitch, the bowline-on-a-bight requires practice to master. The tricky bit is not learning to tie the knot, but in arranging the two double strands at appropriate lengths to clip off at two varying points. Consider this: if two bolts are positioned one above the other, the two double strands of the knot must be of different lengths to accomplish equalization. This is achieved by tying the knot loose, clipping the double strands into the two anchor points, then snugging the knot up accordingly. This sounds more involved than it is, and with a few minutes practice you'll have it.

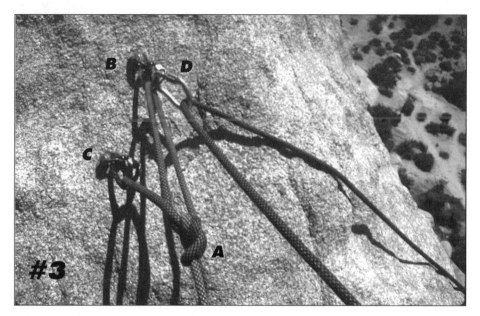

ANCHOR #3: Two-bolt anchor (B and C), tied off with a bowline-on-a-bight (A). Directional on right-hand bolt (D).

PRO: This anchor configuration, known as the "Atomic Clip," is comparatively new and rarely seen. I suspect, however, that as sport climbers become aware of it, it will quickly become the rig of choice for most two-bolt hanging belays that are only outfitted with a fixed system (Quicklinks, chains, etc.). Rock solid, clean and fast to arrange, the Atomic Clip is an example of evolving rigging techniques providing a better way.

CON: This anchor is mono-directional, not multi-directional. The directional at D results in a two-to-one mechanical advantage on only one of the bolts, eliminating the advantage of equalizing in the first place.

COMMENTARY: If you picture yourself standing on a foothold and staring at these two belay bolts, first loosely tie the bowline-on-a-bight and clip both double strands into the two bolts. Next, holding the knot loose, gently pull it side to side till the strands adjust to an equalized length, then snug the knot up. This takes some practice to get both the double strands the desired length, as well as positioning the knot so when the rig is taut you are in a good position in relation to the bolts—not too close and not too far away. Secondly, if one person is doing all the leading on a multi-pitch route, the Atomic Clip is impractical because the lead rope is clipped straight into the bolts. When the second gains the belay, you'd have to unclip the entire rig to anchor the second off, then proceed with the next lead. In other words, the Atomic Rig is favored only if the route is one pitch long, or if you are swinging leads with a partner. Otherwise, too many shenanigans are required.

ANCHOR #4: Sliding knot on sling (C) clipped off at two bolts (A and B). Belayer is tied-off with a clove hitch/locking biner (D), backed up with overhand knot (E) clipped directly into the B bolt. Rope is belayed through directional at F.

PRO: This has become the standard, slick climber's method of rigging a two-bolt sling belay. Note how the C and F slings are both long enough to extend over the slight lip beneath the bolts, so that any abrasion happens to the slings, not the biners or the rope.

CON: The problem is the A bolt, a rusty old ¼″ buttonhead Rawl drive. The directional should be clipped through the equalized point (D), not off a single bolt.

COMMENTARY: This is becoming a likely scenario on old adventure climbs: someone has replaced one of the old "coffin nail" ¼″ bolts with a bomber five-piece Rawl. Ideally, both bolts should be replaced with the newer five-piece Rawls, but there are several reasons this is not always done. First is cost. It shouldn't be, but it is. Climbers don't mind spending the money to retrofit new sport climbs with bombproof anchors, but when repeating old adventure climbs, they are usually satisfied to shore things up to where they are adequate, if only barely. The second, and questionably more important factor, is effort. Electric drilling units are banned in many adventure climbing areas, which means someone has to hand-drill the hole—a big task for the long, five-piece Rawl studs, especially on limestone or granite. All the more reason to equalize the anchor.

#5

SLIDING KNOT

A quick note on the sliding knot aka "sliding X"—the use of the sliding knot is always a judgment call requiring you to take account of several factors.

First, if and when the sliding knot is used as a principal tie-in at the anchor point, it violates our rule of "No Extension" mentioned in our review of SRENE (see page 2 and the sidebar at right). If one of the anchors or components in the system should fail, the system will become slack and drop the climber a short distance, shockloading the remaining anchors.

Second, if the sliding knot is used as one element in a larger, equalized anchor, the failure of one piece means there will be so much slack in the sliding knot that the remaining nut will be unable to absorb any force. Though few rules are fixed in stone, it's almost always best to avoid using the sliding knot alone, as a principal anchor point. The chances and consequences of shockloading are simply too high. Better to use the sliding knot to equalize two less-than-bomber placements, and rig it into a larger, equalized system. (Ref. Rules of Thumb #2.)

SRENE Anchors:

Solid
Redundant
Equalized
No Extension

ANCHOR #6: The Atomic Clip. Bowline-on-a-bight (A) used to tie off a two-bolt sling belay (B and C).

PRO: For lovers of clean, simple rigging, the Atomic Clip is a work of art.

CON: In this instance, if the second falls or has to be lowered, there will likely be some lateral movement of the belayer that could result in the rope abrading on the lip below the bolts—no disaster, since the lip is rounded. Just the same it's always best to have slings grating over a lip, rather than the rope. So here, the sliding knot setup in Anchor #4 on page 16, might be preferred to the Atomic Clip. Lastly, this is not a multi-directional anchor. Lateral movement will shift the force onto one bolt. Since this particular route is straight up and down, the anchor is not subjected to lateral forces; when it is, the Atomic Clip is not a good call. (Ref. Rules of Thumb #5.)

ANCHOR #7: Another look at Anchor #6, the Atomic Clip. The only difference is that a directional figure eight knot (A) has been tied into the climbing rope to belay through.

PRO: This setup, featuring the Atomic Clip (bowline-on-a-bight equalizing a two-bolt sling belay) and a directional figure eight knot to belay through (A), is likely the cleanest method of belaying off two bolts.

CON: This is a new setup requiring expertise with two knots (the bowline-on-a-bight and the directional figure eight) that are commonly used only in rescue work. The Atomic Clip is an improvement over other systems, for any two-bolt sling belay, it eliminates links normally used in the anchor chain. Hence it is worth learning the bowline-on-a-bight. The directional figure eight knot is in fact the

perfect knot to use as a directional to belay through. Its advantages over the overhand knot or the regular figure eight is that it is stronger and is easier to untie after it's been shockloaded, as happens when catching a fall and lowering. As always when using the lead rope to tie off anchors, the drawback is that the rigging eats up rope—not much, but if the next lead is a long one, you might need that extra few feet. Be aware of this possibility. As always when rigging with the lead rope, escape is involved and time consuming if re-rigging is involved.

Belaying off the anchor ("Direct Belay")

As seen, the standard belaying method is to lash yourself to a sound anchor, and then belay through a device attached to your harness, with the climbing rope running through a directional clipped to the anchor point. Another method, used widely by European guides and favored by the AMGA (American Mountain Guides Association), involves clipping the belay device directly into the anchor.

To avoid belaying directly off one piece of gear, equalize the anchor with a cordelette. Per the belay device—either a widemouthed locking biner with a Munter hitch, or a Gri-Gri works best—maximum braking is obtained when both strands of rope (the strand running to and the strand running away from the device) run parallel to each other. To allow easy working of the hitch or Gri-Gri, rig the system so the belay device is clipped to the anchor point at about chest level. You want the device to be in a position where you can reach above and below it (necessary when taking in and paying out rope). If the device is too low, say, you have to bend and reach down to belay and lock the rig off in the event of a fall. When the device is at chest level, belaying is simplified.

Photo: "Direct Belay" consisting of two bolts clipped off with locking biners (A and B), equalized by a cordelette (C). The climber is tied off at D with two biners, gates opposed; the belay is arranged directly off the cordelette at E, featuring a widemouthed biner and a Munter hitch. Note that E—the actual belay point—is rigged at chest-level with the belayer.

Warning: The Direct Belay should never employ a belay plate or tube (like an ATC) because the brake hand must be brought up awkwardly to create the necessary angle on the brake hand side.

PRO: The Direct Belay avoids the need to use a directional, which multiplies the force roughly two times. The Munter hitch is relatively easy to tie off when weighted, and is also a releasable knot when under tension (easily converted to a raising and lowering system). The belayer is also separate from the belay, so once the hitch is tied off and secured, the belayer is no longer shackled to the belay system, and is free to move about or cast off on the next lead.

CON: When you must work to get a bomber belay anchor, and the individual components and placements are set in several cracks—some high, some low, some to the side—the cordelette is not always possible or practical to rig. Because you never want to belay directly off one piece of gear, no matter how bomber it is, the Direct Belay must at the bare minimum be clipped to at least two equalized pieces. When a cordelette can be rigged to equalize all anchor components, the only scenario I can imagine where I would not choose the Direct Belay is if I was on a small stance and was forced to belay off poor anchors. Here, providing the stance was secure enough, I would probably rather have the belay device connected to my harness. If the follower came off, I'd prefer to try and have my body absorb as much of the load as possible, as opposed to having to load shock directly onto a dubious anchor.

A closer look at the anchor point in the photo on page 20.

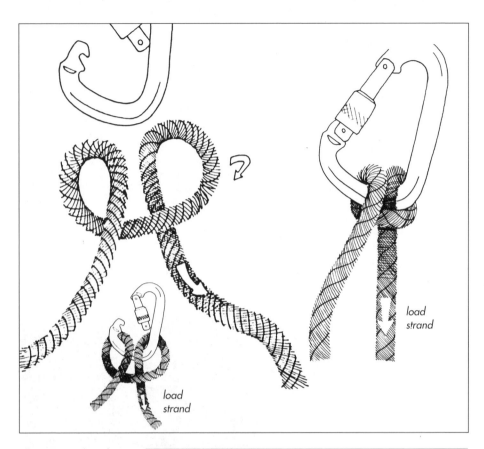

Illustration and text from How To Rock Climb! Knots for Climbers by Craig Luebben (Chockstone Press, 1995).

Munter Hitch

1. Twist two coils into the rope as shown and fold the second coil toward the first.

2. Clip a locking carabiner into both coils. Lock the carabiner. Make sure the Munter Hitch is oriented with the load stand next to the spine of the carabiner.

3. Set this up correctly, because someone's life is on the other end of the rope!

Using the Munter Hitch

Always align the load-bearing strand (going to the climber) with the spine side, not the gate side, of the locking biner.

The Munter hitch will kink the rope unless it is allowed to run loosely through the biner. This does not mean there should be much slack in the hitch, rather that you should avoid pulling the slack in with the brake hand, which naturally crimps the hitch on itself and on the biner. For a toproped climber: gently pull the rope *below* the hitch with the non-brake hand, as the brake hand gently pulls in the slack (never pulling hard enough for the hitch to bind). When belaying a leader, the brake hand gently feeds rope going to the hitch, as the non-brake hand gently pulls the rope out *above* the hitch. The function of this pulling and feeding on both sides is to insure easy action by eliminating the direct weight and friction of the climbing rope on the hitch. When there's no weight on the hitch, it runs smoothly.

Bird's eye view of the Munter Hitch. Notice the widemouthed biner (A), essential gear when using the Munter Hitch.

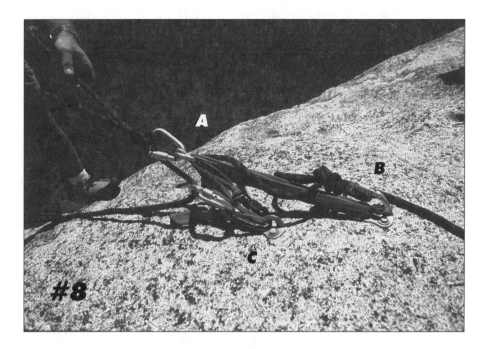

ANCHOR #8: (Above and opposite page) A two-bolt hanging belay on a steep slab. Using a clove hitch, the leader has tied off to a lap link (A) connected to several fixed slings threaded through two bolts (B and C). The weight-bearing tie-in (A) is backed up at B. The belay is arranged so the rope runs through a locking biner at point C, so if the follower should fall, point C will take the brunt of the load, as opposed to the belayer's back.

PRO: The weight-bearing anchor point (A) is equalized between the two bolts (B and C). This is accomplished because the lap link can slide on the sling as the belayer moves side to side, an impossibility if the rope between A and B were taut, hence the slack. Belaying through the bolt (C) is a standard practice on sling belays, particularly on dicey face climbs where falls are routine. (Still, the safer method is to belay through the equalized anchor point.) This setup is compact, functional and quick to rig and break down.

CON: I always try and anchor directly into both bolts. Though both bolt hangers have slings running through them, the biner hole on these modern hangers is large enough to accommodate both the slings and an anchor biner, as at point C. The biner at point A should be flipped over so the gate cannot contact the rock. As a general rule, always employ carabiners in the same fashion; down and out (i.e. with a "D" shape carabiner, the large end down with the gate away from the rock). These few adjustments would improve this setup.

COMMENTARY: This type of setup is seen frequently at sport climbing areas, where a belay also doubles as a rappel station. The newer and now standard ⅜″ and ½″ bolts are so strong that—properly placed—concern about them failing is often considered a non-issue. This is not a good concept. Bolts do fail, so never blindly trust any bolt no matter how good it looks. The issue here, as always, is the fixed slings. Slings are always left behind because someone rapped off the anchor. Without the lap-link, the ropes would have been dragged over the slings, which melts the nylon and weakens it drastically. The lap-link gets around this problem, but it does not decrease the slings exposure to UV rays, nor does it halt the natural abrasion of the slings where they run through the bolt hangers. Always inspect the slings before trusting them for either a belay or a rappel. Once the slings feel brittle, they are no longer strong enough to use. A problem here is—how do you untie them? A lot of use will cinch the knot so tight it may have to be cut away. If this proves impossible, use the bolts as if the slings were not there at all.

ANCHOR #9: Three-bolt hanging belay (slab) equalized with a cordelette. The belayer is anchored in with one rope, and is belaying with another that runs through the lowest bolt (C).

PRO: The bolts are spread out in a way that would require more gear and several cluttered systems to equalize—if not for the cordelette, which simplifies everything. The belayer is clipped off to the cordelette with two biners, gates opposed (D), and the directional through which he is belaying (C) is a $^3/_8''$ bolt, while the upper two bolts (B and C) are the old $^1/_4''$ Rawl Drive bolts. In the event of an emergency, this setup is easy to escape from.

CON: Two of the bolts are untrustworthy quarter-inchers; but sometimes climbers are faced with less than ideal anchors and must—and usually can—compensate with crafty rigging. Some climbers disagree with me here, saying you can always downclimb, thus avoiding having to belay from questionable anchors. Not so. I've been caught in numerous situations where the only way off was up, and the available anchors were dreadful. Here, the cordelette turned a potentially tense belay into a bombproof one. Though the cordelette is easy to rig, it takes practice to get the system as perfectly arranged as the set up featured here.

Remember, for lead changes and to facilitate clipping and unclipping from individual components of the belay, a comfortable body position—neither too close to the anchors, nor too far below them—is desired at all hanging belays. If the cordelette is too long, you may have to tie additional knots at the tie-in point to shorten it; but your body position relative to the anchors is principally accomplished by how much or how little rope runs between the tie-in knot on your harness (point D on the cordelette).

Strictly speaking, a cordelette is not a multi-directional system, meaning that if the belay was impacted directly from one or the other side, more stress would be placed on one of the bolts and less stress on the others. This is not so crucial with bolts, which when properly set in good rock are strong enough in all directions (excepting the two $\frac{1}{4}''$ bolts here), but when the separate points of an anchor are less than desired, a more complicated multi-directional system is a wiser and safer choice. (Ref. Rules of Thumb #4.)

Slings are often invaluable in rigging an anchor, particularly when equalizing several components of a multi-component anchoring matrix. Aside from the fundamental issues previously discussed in *How To Rock Climb: Climbing Anchors*, the business of "close" and "narrow angles" should be understood. This issue has been taken up countless times before, but all the baffling graphs and figures have often provided us with more confusion than insight. The engineer is satisfied with nothing short of a dissertation, while the practical climber simply wants rules of thumb. But here, rules of thumb are not enough. You must know the why of the matter as well. In simple terms, it works like this:

Whenever a sling is used to connect two pieces of protection, you end up with a triangular configuration. The points of the triangle are comprised of the left-hand placement (A), the right-hand placement (B), and the point at which you secure the sling to the climbing rope—the anchor point (C). The triangle can be visualized as a piece of pie. All triangles and all pieces of pie form a "V": the branches of the sling coming from the left-hand placement (A) and the right-hand placement (B) converge like a "V" at the anchor point (C). The critical thing to grasp here concerns the angle of this "V." You don't need to work out the vexing mathematics involved, and involved charts and figures will confuse all but the math students. Simply understand that the bigger the angle formed by this "V"—the bigger the wedge of pie, if you will—the greater the force placed on the A and B placements. Again, as the angle of the "V" increases, so do the forces placed on the placements. This phenomenon is known as "load multiplication," and it's sobering to see how quickly the forces increase as the angle of the "V" increases (as the piece of pie gets bigger).

Consider this: imagine a two-bolt belay. If a 1,000 lb. force was applied to the anchor point (C), and the "V" formed by the sling was at 20 degrees, a load of about 500 lbs. would be placed on each bolt. At 40 degrees, the force increases to 540 lbs.; at 80 degrees, about 710 lbs.; at 120 degrees, a load of 1,000

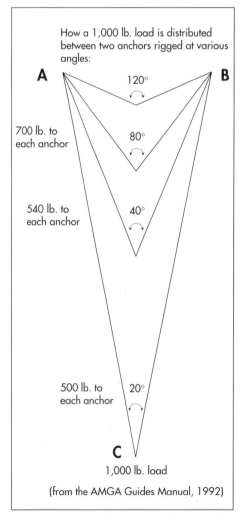

How a 1,000 lb. load is distributed between two anchors rigged at various angles:

A   120°   B

700 lb. to   80°
each anchor

540 lb. to   40°
each anchor

500 lb. to   20°
each anchor

C

1,000 lb. load

(from the AMGA Guides Manual, 1992)

pounds is placed on each bolt. This tells us that the comfort zone is when the angle of the "V" is at 40 degrees or less. The caution zone is between 40 and 80 degrees, and the danger zone is anything over 80 degrees, where the forces are multiplied exponentially.

This information gives us rule of thumb: whenever connecting two placements with a sling, strive to keep the angle of the V (at the anchor point) around thirty degrees, and never over sixty degrees. (Some guides tell students to try and keep the angle of the V less than 90 degrees, but this is pushing the system too far for my skin.) The reason we normally connect two placements with a sling is to equalize potential forces between both placements. If the radical angle of the triangular configuration formed by the sling actually increases the load on each placement, you've done yourself more harm than good and have defeated the concept of equalizing the load.

Of course, we can only take what the rock affords, and many times it's necessary to place nuts rather far apart (which creates the high angles) and connect them with a sling. The only immediate solution here is to use longer slings to decrease the angle of the V, to narrow that wedge of pie. Remember, the closer the anchor point (C) is to the individual placements (A and B), the larger the angle of the V, and the greater load multiplication. The thinner the slice of pie, the less force each placement will have to bear.

R. Garibotti, D. French
climbing in Eldorado, CO.
Photo: Beth Wald.

Nuts

First ascents, traditional free climbs and big walls all require expertise in placing nuts to secure protection and arrange belay anchors. As covered in *How To Rock Climb: Climbing Anchors* (the first anchors book), and as we will see in the following chapter, a handful of rigging systems are suitable for almost all anchoring matrices, providing you are flexible and can improvise on a theme. The sliding knot, cordelette, and the crafty use of slings and clove hitches remain the basic rigging tools to equalize complex multi-nut anchors. However, as time goes by, the use of these tools and the methods of integrating them into a clean and unified anchor are refined as more climbers put more thought and apply more experience to the task. Old techniques, once acceptable, are replaced by safer, easier, more bombproof (SEB) methods. This is especially true with belay anchors rigged off suspect nuts. Only when the nuts have been equalized to exploit their last ounce of strength can you lean back and belay without fretting that the whole Magilla will blow out and cast you onto Jordan's Bank. Exploiting the strength of bunk nuts is always a matter of rigging, of equalizing the various components into a unified whole. I have mentioned it several times and I'll mention it again: it is not feasible to show a hundredth of the possible multi-nut setups you'll routinely face on adventure climbs. We can only show examples of typical setups. Do not memorize, rather study the various setups, consider options and mentally formulate ways you might do things differently.

ANCHOR #10: An "anchor" consisting of two wired tapers (A and B) connected with a sling (C).

PRO: Though the nuts are hidden in the crack, both A and B are perfect, bottleneck placements so secure that even this horribly rigged system would probably not fail.

CON: Though this was used as an anchor, it is definitely not one. It is also a perfect example of poorly rigging two bombproof nuts. When the sling is weighted, this system actually increases the inward forces against the nuts, which is not so much a problem here, though it's uncommon that you get nuts as solid as these. Try and avoid any system that places a bad angle of outward pull on the individual placements. Lastly, understand that while you often must add an opposing piece to achieve better multidirectional security, the opposing piece will usually add more resultant force to each piece.

ANCHOR #11 (opposite): Same as Anchor #10, but clove hitches (A and B) have been tied directly into the two nuts to eliminate undesirable angles of pull on the placements.

PRO: Not only do the clove hitches allow the sling to maintain an optimum angle of pull on the nuts, but so long as some little pressure is placed on the anchor, inward forces between A and B keep each nut well set. This is one of the best ways to rig two opposing wired nuts in a horizontal crack, a scenario not uncommon on traditional ("trad") adventure climbs.

CON: While the force on these pieces is minimized by this rigging, whenever you're opposing nuts in a horizontal crack, the overall security of the anchor is the question. Sometimes

you must increase the resultant forces in order to decrease the chance that they'll fall out—meaning that if the nuts were less bomber, tucked back in a bottleneck, and without bottleneck placements, nuts in a horizontal crack or prone to wiggle loose, the sliding knot (which if weighted directly will keep the nuts pulling against one another, holding each other in place) might be more appropriate. The biggest problem The biggest problem with this anchor is that it consists of only two nuts, which only a madman would call safe. This should be looked at and studied as protection, not as an anchor.

COMMENTARY: The only potential problem in rigging such a system is that some people have not taken the time to learn the subtleties of working with the clove hitch, and unless the clove hitch is properly tied and cinched tight, it can fail— same with all knots. Consider attaching a sling and a biner to a bedpost (or some other stationary "anchor" in your home), and using a short length of rope/sling, take a half an hour and teach yourself just how the knot works. First, learn how to get the knot tight. Observe that after you have twisted the two loops into the hitch, you must pull on both ends to cinch the knot tight enough so it will not slip when pulled in either direction. Next is to learn how to feather the knot when it is loose, till you get it in precisely the spot you want it, then knowing how to cinch it tight and keeping it in exactly the same spot. This second part—learning how to feather the hitch and cinching it snug in exactly the desired spot—is fundamental to rigging perfectly equalized anchors (as with Anchor #11). Also make sure the load-bearing strand of the knot is aligned as closely to the spine of the carabiner as possible. This is especially important when using a fat rope and tying clove hitches onto big, pear-shaped biners. Otherwise, it's easy to create unnecessary leverage on the biner. Once you master the clove hitch, it quickly becomes an invaluable tool. But if you do not have experience with the clove hitch, it can quickly become a liability. Though not a concern with good webbing, be aware that clove hitches slightly weaken the sling.

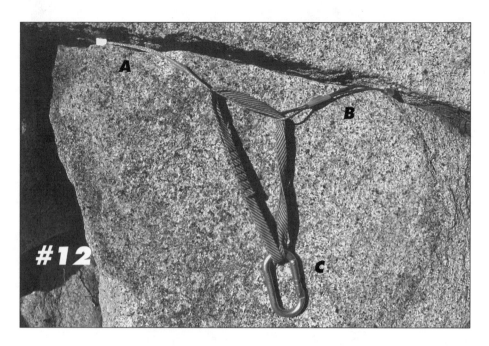

ANCHOR #12: Two nuts (A and B) strung together with a Quickdraw and clipped off at C.

PRO: There is nothing to recommend this "anchor" whatsoever.

CON: Of the many viable methods of rigging opposing nuts in a horizontal crack, this is not one of them. The most glaring error is threading the Spectra runner directly through the wires, a tactic that can result in a sliced runner. The B nut is clearly marginal, and the slightest outward force—which is inevitable when this system is loaded—will rip B from the crack, shockload A, which will certainly fail when stressed directly outward, and the climbing team will thence spend three freezing winters in purgatory for recklessness. As is, this setup is unsatisfactory even as a component of a larger anchor. Granted, it is necessary to know how to safely retreat leaving the least amount of gear behind, but this example is not the method.

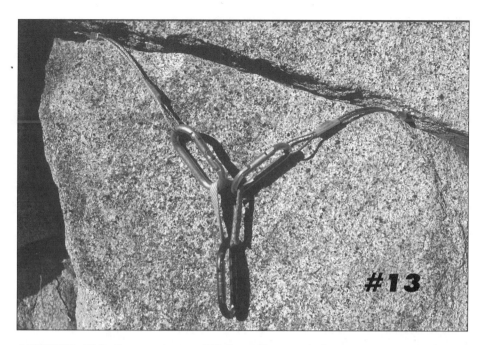

ANCHOR #13: Same setup as #12 (opposite page), but properly rigged with biners clipped through the nuts, rather than a sling threaded through them.

PRO: This is a standard and relatively effective setup for closely spaced wired nuts in a horizontal crack.

CON: This is far from bombproof, but adequate as a component of a larger anchor system. As is, it is too marginal to make up a complete anchor. One of the problems is the nuts cannot be placed so they are tucked back in a bottleneck, and without bottleneck placements, nuts in a horizontal crack are prone to move from their original berth unless rigged so they are under constant pressure. Here, the nuts are so close together it is impossible. The second problem is that they are set so close together it is impossible to rig them off so they are in constant pressure against one another—which helps keep them set in their optimum position. The close spacing of the nuts cannot be helped. You can only go with what the rock affords, and this rig makes good use of rather slim pickings. As protection, this is adequate. As an anchor it is not, for the whole shebang actually consists of one piece of pro (no redundancy).

ANCHOR #14: Self-equalizing system with two anchors at each end: Two wired tapers (A), a small SLCD (B), a Tri-Cam (C), all connected and equalized by a sling (D) featuring the sliding knot.

PRO: Excepting the Tri-Cam, which looks funky (but they often do), all the placements are solid. The D sling that connects the placements provides a functional and self-equalizing multi-directional setup.

CON: As mentioned earlier, whenever you couple two placements with biners (as is done here with the two wires on the left, and the SLCD and Tri-Cam on the right), it is virtually impossible for the forces to be shared equally between the placements.

With A, one wire has to be only the slightest bit lower for the other to absorb the majority of the force. One-sixteenth of an inch of difference is all that it takes. Here we can see that the left-hand wire (in A) extends further down than the other, and the darker sling coming off the Tri-Cam has a little slack in it. Anyway, connecting two pieces of pro with one biner (or even doubled biners, as with A) is standard and kosher if both pieces, and the anchor as a whole, is stout as a live oak. But if the placements are less than spectacular, consider clipping off the pieces individually, and equalizing them against other components in the anchor matrix. (Ref. Rules of Thumb #2.)

The D sling, with its sliding knot, has its advantages, especially when the direction of pull changes—meaning that the anchor will be variously pulled on from down and left and down and right. The drawback is, first, there is no redundancy, and second, if either grouping of nuts fail, the anchor point will drop the distance of the branch/strand beneath the failed grouping, and will shockload onto the remaining group. Here, the strand beneath the A wires is easily a foot long, so if A fails, the whole Magilla drops a foot and shockloads onto B and C. It is crucial to understand that the sliding knot allows lateral movement, which can render poor pieces worthless. Everything depends on the direction of pull. I personally avoid using the sliding knot as the principal anchor point, unless A), the direction of pull will not cause lateral movement in the system, B) the placements are so dicey they must be self-equalized at all times, or C), there seems no chance at all that any of the placements will fail.

I find that the sliding knot is most useful in equalizing components of an anchor, then connecting said components with a cordelette; or, in the case of a multi-pitch route (as opposed to a toprope anchor like this), tying straight into them using clove hitches on the lead rope.

ANCHOR #15: (Below) Three wired nuts (A, C, and D), equalized with Quickdraws.

PRO: Though not visible, each of the nuts are bombproof, which is always the principal consideration in constructing an

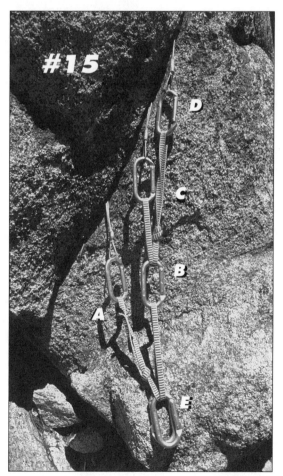

anchor. The hardest part of equalizing any system without a pulley-type rig running between the individual nuts, is to rig the slings at just the right length so (in this instance) when the system is weighted at E, the force is equal on all three nuts. Here, overhand knots have been tied in the Quickdraws from nuts A and C. The knots are cleverly tied so that if nuts A or D were to fail, they would minimize the shockloading at points B or C. Note that all the biners are positioned so the gates will open down and away from the rock.

CON: This is not a multi-directional anchor, and is sound only for a downward pull. It is virtually impossible to perfectly equalize any anchor using straight slings because one can never get the lengths exactly right. This is acceptable here because all three nuts are very sound, and the system is rigged so if one nut fails, there will be no shockloading on the system. (Ref. Rules of Thumb #5)

COMMENTARY: Personally, when I run into such a setup as

this, I often tie the rope straight into A, C, and D, using a figure eight-on-a-bight on top (D), and equalizing the nut with the others by using clove hitches at C and A. This eliminates the need for the slings. The drawbacks are that there is no easy escape, changeovers between belayer and leader are far more complicated, and whenever you tie the anchor off directly with the rope you never have true equalization. All of these factors underscore the fact that specific situations and usage must always be taken into account for every anchor. The reason I would normally tie off with the climbing rope is that I typically climb with a skilled leader and we swing leads, I am rarely in a situation where imminent escape is a consideration (though you never know for certain), and while the climbing rope cannot achieve true equalization, I can usually get such bombproof nuts that a more involved rigging system is unnecessary for the simple reason that the one I have will never fail. Lastly, if this anchor was for a multi-pitch climb, rather than a one-pitch crack route, I'd add an opposing upward component for added security, especially important for belaying the leader above.

ANCHOR #16: (On left.) Double self-equalizing. Though hard to see, A is comprised of two small hexes. Both B and C are mid-range tapers. The sling connected to biner A goes down to the tie-in biner D, then up to E. The sling connected to biner B goes down and through the doubled biners at E, then back up to C. Photo on right: Overhand knot used to eliminate shockloading in photo on left (knot slightly weakens the sling).

PRO: All the nuts are bombproof, and by using the "sliding knot" at D and E, the system is well equalized for a downward pull. Potential for shockloading decreased by using two nuts at A.

CON: There is no redundancy in this system. It's also a little ornate for my taste. The system is too elongated by the slings. With bombproof nuts like these, we could streamline things by tying the rope directly into the nuts, using clove hitches to equalize. And without a directional for an upward pull, this setup has too much play in it, regardless of how well it is equalized. Though not often, belayers can get dragged laterally on a belay stance when the second falls, and a sharp sideways jolt on this system could be dangerous. Easily fixed by slotting a couple directionals for upward force.

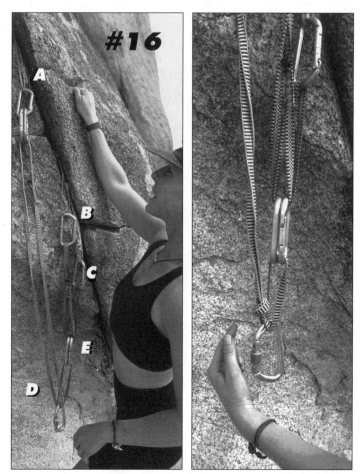

Wolfgang Gullich on
Your Mother 5.13a,
Eldorado Canyon
Photo: Beth Wald

Cordelettes

As mentioned, the cordelette (usually a 20-foot length of 7mm Perlon—though some climbers prefer 6mm, others, 8mm) has only recently come into its own as a practical tool in quickly and efficiently equalizing the various components of an anchoring matrix. The majority of belay anchors feature fair to good placements that are relatively quick to secure. The following examples show the cordelette at work when the placements are relatively sound and involved rigging is unnecessary.

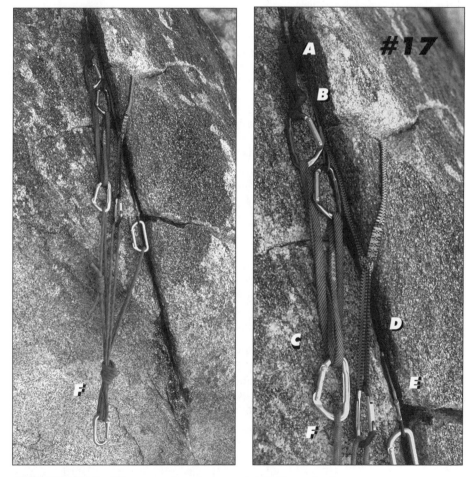

ANCHOR #17: (Close-up of anchor on right) Two wired tapers (A and B) equalized by a Spectra sling (C) configured with the sliding knot; a sling over a horn; a small three-cam SLCD (E). All three components of the anchor are tied off to a cordelette (F).

PRO: The rigging is sound, but the best asset of this anchor is the B taper, which is absolutely bombproof. Note the slip knot in the D sling, which helps cinch the sling over the horn and inhibits the sling's movement when the system is weighted.

CON: This is a good example of where the cordelette is not at its best. It simply puts too much play in the system. A shorter cordelette would reduce the play, but excepting the sling over the horn (D), the other placements are rock solid and don't really benefit from being equalized against one another. Also, excepting the D sling, the other slings are unnecessary; the placements could be clipped off straight to the cordelette.

Equalizing (C) is usually a sound practice with any anchor, but when the rock has to break away for the individual nuts to fail, it may be unnecessary. Simpler and faster to tie the lead rope straight into the placements—figure eight-on-a-bight on top, and clove hitches on down. Of course, without a directional for an upward pull, this anchor is only satisfactory to belay a climber up to it, not past it, where upward force could conceivably lift the belayer off the stance and the nuts from the crack. In short: a directional placed below the anchor point not only safeguards against upward forces, but eliminates play in the system—so long as the directional is rigged taut against the anchor point. The problem is

The problem is that there is no crack below the anchor point, so as is, a directional is unobtainable.

COMMENTARY: It cannot be overstated: crafty rigging can exploit the last ounce of strength from marginal anchors, and poor rigging can greatly compromise the brawn of good protection. But a sound anchor is always based on the security of the individual nuts, SLCDs, pitons and bolts. Rigging techniques have come so far in twenty years one could get the impression that given the right setup , any old nuts will do. This philosophy will kill you. A sound anchor always starts with good individual placements. Period.

ANCHOR #18 (opposite): A toprope anchor consisting of two hexes (A and B) equalized by a sling/sliding knot (C), a hex (D) and a sling around a sapling (E, and out of view), also equalized by a sling/sliding knot, both groupings connected and equalized by a third sling/sliding knot (G).

PRO: This toprope anchor protects a slab route that wanders, meaning that at various points, a climber will be somewhat left or right of the overhead toprope anchor. Should he/she fall when not directly below the anchor, a slightly oblique force will be put on the anchor. For this reason, a completely self-equalizing system like this one allows for limited lateral adjusting. That is, you can yank on this anchor from several angles and it will adjust accordingly.

CON: The hazards of any completely self-equalizing system is the potential for shockloading if one of the placements should fail. The safeguard is to make certain that each placement is A1. Perhaps both the A and B hexes are bomber, but when slotted endwise like this, the tolerances are so minimal that a sharp angular tug can blow them out of the crack. If this happens, the system will collapse and shockload onto the right-hand (D and E) nuts, the anchor actually dropping the distance of one or the other branches/strands of the G cordelette. Toproping might not result in the forces generated by a big leader fall, but lowering a climber off can stress the anchor significantly. Many times a belayer does not lower a climber soft as church music, rather he lets him down in fits and starts, sometimes locking up the belay device altogether, particularly once the climber is near the ground. Each stop and start shockloads the belay anchor with force far exceeding the climbers

weight, and the anchor sees two times that force—yet another reason to lower smoothly. And if you're using a fully self-equalizing system like this one, make certain all of the placements are rock solid. By replacing sling G with a cordelette or with a double-length Spectra runner tied off with an overhand loop, the potential shockloading is minimized and the anchor would still be self-equalizing. Toproping anchors are often out of sight and temporarily out of mind. The added security of an upward directional, if not imperative, lends a peace of mind. (Ref. Rules of Thumb #6.)

COMMENTARY: Understand that the following practices will greatly increase the force an anchor must withstand: lowering at speed and then quickly stopping; toproping with static ropes (which do not stretch), whereas the anchor—rather than the dynamic qualities of a lead rope—must absorb the total impact force—when a climber falls with slack in the line and when raising/winching a climber while hangdogging.

ANCHOR #19: (Above) A TCU or three-cam unit (A), two SLCDs joined with one sling (B), two more SLCDs equalized with a sling utilizing the sliding knot, all connected with a cordelette (D).

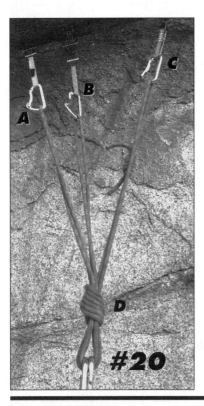

PRO: Most of the SLCDs are pretty sound.

CON: Among several large errors in this system, the most glaring is B, for if one or the other SLCD blows, the other is no good either. C is properly equalized, but if either nut goes, there will be too much slack in the sling for the cordelette to weight the remaining SLCD. Better to clove hitch the SLCDs with individual slings. Another problem is that the angle is pretty wide on the cordelette; however without B, the angle between A and C nears 90 degrees, so B actually reduces the resultant forces (but note how the A branch is loose). Since this system is not multi-directional, the quality and appropriateness of this anchor depends entirely on it's intended use. For straight down, in-line force, this anchor may work; for lateral forces, this anchor spells tragedy.

COMMENTARY: This arrangement points out one of the potential problems with the cordelette, the purpose of which is to equalize various components of the anchor. When said components (here, the SLCDs) are themselves equalized with slings (as with B and C), if one of the placements fails, the cordelette can not self-adjust because its dimensions are fixed.

ANCHOR #20: (opposite on bottom) Three SLCDs, equalized by a cordelette (D).

PRO: This is a revised and simplified setup of Anchor #19, featuring narrower angles on the SLCDs.

CON: Though not visible, the middle SLCD (B) is not particularly sound, and the other two (A and C) are only adequate. The rigging on this system is an improvement of Anchor #19, but the overall might of the anchor is less than ideal. And remember, while the tight grouping of placements means narrower angles, it also means that the anchor is less of a directional than it would be if the placements were more spread out. As is, this anchor is good only for a straight, downward pull. Remember, the cordelette is not multi-directional no matter what the angles are. Also, using less pieces of pro, simply to reduce the angles, is normally a poor tradeoff.

ANCHOR #21: (Below) Another variation of Anchor #19, featuring five SLCDs, equalized by a cordelette.

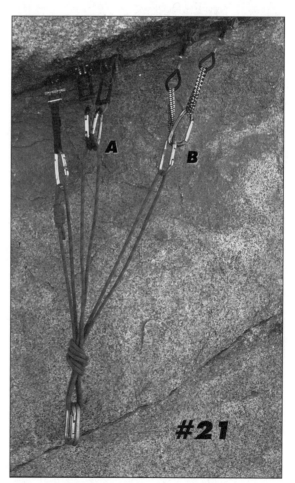

PRO: This is an attempt to make the best of a bad situation by attempting to rig the system so that if a placement(s) fails, there will be no shockloading on the other placements. Note how two SLCDs are clipped through the middle branch of the cordelette at A, and how at B, the right-hand SLCD is clipped into the biner of the SLCD to its immediate left. For either one of these configurations to actually work—for the forces to be equally shared between the two SLCDs at both A and B—the tolerances have to be exactly right. A quarter-of-an-inch of play in either A or B means one of the SLCDs will be absorbing far more force than the other.

CON: This anchor is dicey because the SLCDs are all placed in a shallow, horizontal flare, and not one of them is absolutely bombproof. Also, to go with inferior placements simply to reduce the angles on the cordelette is a dangerous practice.

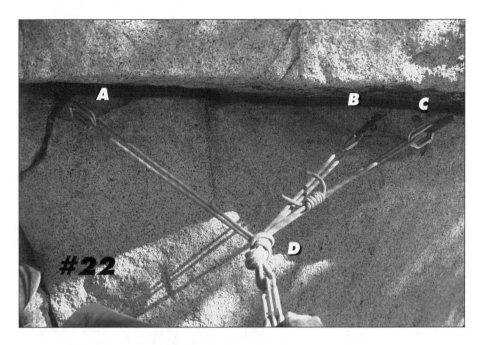

ANCHOR #22: Multi-directional cordelette (for multi-pitch route) rigged off three SLCDs (A, B and C).

PRO: There are other ways to rig these three nuts, but none so simply and efficiently places, and keeps, the direction of pull consistent on the nuts in their optimum position. Just the same, this system is not truly multi-directional.

CON: The angle on the two widest points (A and C) is about 120 degrees. Theoretically, if a straight outward force of 1,000 lbs were applied, anchor A and C would both be loaded to 1,000 lbs. each. By narrowing the angle, the forces would decrease (see chart and discussion on page 28).

COMMENTARY: With this setup, or any featuring nuts in a horizontal crack, an equalizing system such as the sliding knot is often used. This can sometimes stress the placements in a way that may cause them to shift. The cordelette eliminates that concern. Equalizing this system depends on where the knot is tied at D. If the knot is tied so it sits either to the left or to the right of its current position, the direction of pull will change on the individual placements. So when rigging the cordelette, when you draw the branches together to tie them off, give a tug and make sure the system weights the protection in the optimum direction—that is, in the direction that the nut can withstand the greatest force. This might sound abstruse, but once you ponytail the thing together at point D, just put a finger or biner through the loop and slide it side to side and observe what happens to the direction of pull on the nuts—and all will be clear instantly.

ANCHOR 23: Toprope anchor consisting of a SLCD (A); two wired tapers in opposition (B); a sling, featuring the sliding knot (C) that equalizes A and B, and is clipped into a cordelette (F); two SLCDs (D and E), both clipped into the cordelette.

PRO: This is as close to a masterpiece of simple, clean engineering as you are apt to ever see. The nuts are sound, the rigging plain and straightforward. Note the position of the biners—all gates are up, away from the rock.

CON: Aside from not being multi-directional, the only negative about this setup is that the cordelette runs over a lip at F. Because this is a toprope anchor, climbers will certainly be lowering off of it, and if the climb is stiff, falls are likely. Falling and lowering on any kind of anchor causes flex in the system, and here, the inevitable result is that when the anchor is weighted and unweighted, the figure eight knot at F will saw on the edge beneath it—not enough to sever the cordelette, but it takes surprisingly little sawing action to wear a hole through the sheath of any kind of rope—even a static line like this one.

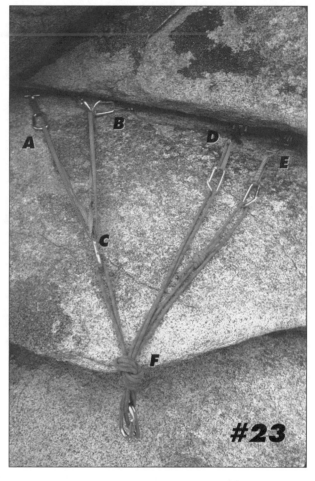

The solution is to tie the cordelette off perhaps a foot higher, and extend the anchor over the lip with several doubled slings. Always extend the tie-in point over the lip, so any sawing action does not occur on the climbing rope.

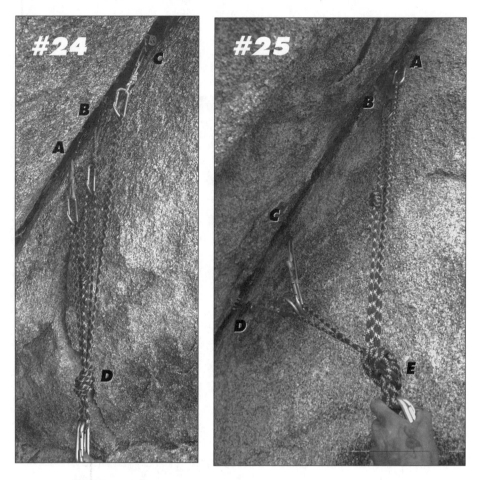

ANCHOR #24: (Above left.) Three bombproof SLCDs (A, B and C) equalized by a cordelette (D).

PRO: Although possible to simplify this setup by eliminating the cordelette and tying directly into the SLCDs, as it is, the placements are so far above the belay ledge that the cordelette makes things a little more manageable.

CON: Because all three SLCDs are so closely spaced and are set to withstand force in the same direction (straight down), any lateral movement at the tie in (D) could cause the SLCDs to shift, though probably not very much. SLCDs can normally shift quite a bit in the crack and still remain sound, but if you cause the placements to shift one direction and shockload them in another direction, they can fail. This is alarmist talk with this particular system, which is good for direct, downward forces. In fact, nice, narrow angles are usually best—providing the system does not allow the individual pieces to shift when weighted in any direction.

ANCHOR #25: (Above right.) A wired taper (A), and three SLCDs (B, C and D) equalized with a cordelette (E).

PRO: This is a rearrangement of Anchor #24. By moving the C and D down from the higher group, a multi-directional anchor is accomplished.

CON: By moving C down, the downward strength is decreased. Better to add another piece. Though this system is multi-directional, it is not multi-directional equalized. This means that while you can pull the anchor from various angles, doing so will place the load on individual pieces, as opposed to the pieces collectively absorbing the force.

ANCHOR #26: (Above right.) Another toprope anchor rigged at the same place as Anchor #18 (reproduced on the left, see also pages 42-43), consisting of two SLCDs (A and B), a wired taper (C), equalized with a cordelette.

PRO: Just about everything with this system is superior to Anchor #25. Less gear, better placements, and no chance for shockloading if one of the placements fail. The utility of the cordelette should be pretty obvious by now.

CON: This system is good only for a direct, downward pull. That means as the tie in (D) moves side to side—as inevitably happens when you're toproping a wandering pitch—one branch/strand of the cordelette goes slack and the opposite branch bears any and all force. The easy solution is to slot a directional (for upward pull) somewhere beneath D, to keep it from moving.

ANCHOR #27: Two tapers (A and C), a sling over a flake (B), connected together with a cordelette.

PRO: The only thing to recommend this belay is that the sling (B) over the flake is solid for a downward pull (only).

CON: A good example when the cordelette is a poor choice (though the cordelette is not the only problem here). Downward force will load A and C at the wrong angles relative to the way the nuts are set, and A, at the very least, would likely fail. Much better to forego A completely, move the knot at D closer to C (to reduce the oblique angle of pull), and concentrate on shoring up this anchor by exploiting the crack below the C taper, possibly setting up a self-equalizing system off a couple small wires and a big SLCD in the flare with the shadow in the back. It's hard to say, but this much is for certain: as is, this anchor is no better than the sling at B, which in the absence of a directional below somewhere, is very susceptible to an upward force stripping it right off the flake and hurling the climbing team to the Other Side.

The Shield, *El Capitan*
Photo: Beth Wald

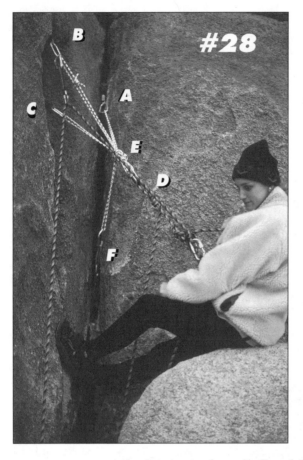

ANCHOR #28: Four SLCDs (A, B, C, and F). F is directional for an upward pull, and when tied together with the cordelette (E), the entire system is multi-directional. The belay rope (D) is clipped through the B placement to form a directional.

PRO: Good example of the cordelette simplifying a system that would otherwise involve many extra slings and biners to connect and equalize the four placements.

CON: The directional (D) is clipped through only one SLCD. This is especially dire if the placement is less than great, as the force of the falling follower will be roughly multiplied by two. (As a standard practice, always run the directional (D) directly through the equalized anchor point (E).) It is not so crucial that the directional (F) be good to 5,000 pounds, for its main purpose is to equalize the direction of pull on the placements above (A, B and C), and to safeguard against a stiff upward pull—which is possible only if the leader passes this anchor, climbs above and takes a mammoth whistler generating enough force to yank the maiden off her perch and up into the air. This is improbable, particularly in a crack, where pro is commonly at hand. But the point is: sometimes the directional that safeguards against an upward pull must absorb some force, so said directional should always be more than ornamental. (Ref. Rules of Thumb #4.)

COMMENTARY: To thoroughly understand any of this, mentally go through all the steps of constructing the anchor yourself. To assist in that process, let's walk through this particular system step by step. First, the leader gains the ledge/seat and either decides, or is constrained by lack of rope, to belay right there. After deciding that she wants to sit on the ledge, with her feet braced against the opposite wall, she scours the two cracks above for the most bombproof placements. This is the always the first step—secure the best placements. It is (typically) easier to organize the system if the placements are reasonably close to each other, but always go after the strongest placements no matter where they are. Here, the leader has placed two SLCDs in the right crack (A and F), and two in the left one (B and C). After these are set, she clips the cordelette through the biners connected to each placement, creating the branches of the system by drawing together the slack between the pieces till she had a tentative hub, roughly at point E. With her fingers separating the various branches/strands, she can pull slightly and see how the system responds when weighted, moving the hub/center around by letting the strands slide through a carabiner she has clipped into all the loops. The notion is to try and get the strands to weight the placements in their optimum direction of pull, in an attitude that they will not shift. This is a very simple, quick, and self-explanatory process once you try it. When the optimum center/hub has

been determined, she will tie the knot at E, making sure to keep all of the strands taut as she does so. Next she will adjust her direct tie in (to her harness) so when she is seated, her weight will place some little tension in the system to keep things snug—not so tight as to be uncomfortable, and not so loose that there's play in the system. Lastly, she will set up her belay device, and clip a directional Quickdraw (D) directly into the equalized anchor point (E), not simply through one nut in the system, as she's done here (through the B placement). This whole process can be accomplished in several minutes providing you have experience in placing protection, understand the concepts and have some experience in rigging such a system. Every anchor differs, if only slightly, but the same procedures and steps are normally taken in construction every anchor. Practice makes perfect.

ANCHOR #29: (Above) The leader has led through the Anchor #28 setup. It is here that the climbers would most benefit from running the lead rope through the equalized anchor point, rather than simply through one component of the anchor.

The Shield, *El Capitan.*
Photo: Beth Wald

Miscellaneous Anchors

It is futile to try and predict how often you will have to construct anchors from less than ideal, even risky placements. Each climbing area varies according to the geological character of the cracks. But no matter where you climb, you're bound to encounter anchoring setups that require sophisticated rigging techniques to achieve any kind of security. Thin, shallow, horizontal cracks present especially difficult challenges in fashioning bombproof anchors. Here, and in other cases, half a dozen or more rigging techniques might be required in constructing an anchor consisting of groups of equalized placements, each group being equalized by the master/overall system.

The following examples show how separate, overlapping systems work in one anchoring matrix. It is unacceptable to simply memorize the examples. The idea is to show instances of what does and does not work in terms of systems. To familiarize yourself with the systems employed, study the individual setups and get a feel and understanding for how various rigging structures can work in concert with others to build a good belay from sketchy placements.

If you climb somewhere besides a sport climbing area, or desire to climb a longer route, you'll invariably have to fashion belay anchors from less than textbook placements. It is here that rigging/equalizing skills are indispensable.

ANCHOR #30: Anchor for belaying a second—a pitch below—up to this ledge. A, B, and C (all SLCDs), equalized by the cordelette (D), form a multidirectional anchor in the horizontal crack. A triangulation on the rope is accomplished by the directional nut at the belayer's feet (F), which is tied off taut with a clove hitch, and goes up to a locking biner on the belayer's harness. The belay rope passes through a directional at E—to reduce upward pull on belayer—then goes back down to the second climber below.

PRO: This setup employs many of the best anchoring concepts in a simple, straightforward way that is easy to rig and break down. The cordelette notwithstanding, the system uses no special gear—just nuts and biners.

CON: The C branch of the cordelette is a little loose, which means when the rig was tied off at D, the belayer did not first apply a little tug to the system to insure everything was not only taut, but that when weighted, the forces were absorbed by the nuts in their optimum position. The second problem is the belayer's body position. There is perhaps six inches too little rope between D and the belayer's harness. This requires that he stand too erect, for unless he wants to straddle the line coming up from the oppositional F, he can't lean back; and if he can't lean back at least a bit, his legs can't act as shock absorbers if and when the second climber should fall. Because he has rigged a directional (E) to belay through, if the second falls, the force will pull him toward the anchor, and unless he can lean back a little, he could conceivably topple forward when the second comes onto the rope.

COMMENTARY: Looks complicated, but is easy to rig. This is a belay that should be studied, for though involved, the rigging is clean and easy to understand if you take the time to notice and appreciate the principles involved.

The following sequence (Anchors #31 through #34) illustrate four different systems arranged at the same anchor station.

ANCHOR #31: Two small wired tapers (A and B) equalized by a sling/sliding knot (H), a wired taper (C) and a TCU (D) connected via clove hitches tied into a runner (G), two SLCDs (E and F), clipped to one biner and into clove hitch on the climbing rope (I). The climbing rope runs through a directional at J.

PRO: A comprehensive setup that maximizes slender options. H is good use of the sliding knot. G is ideal use of clove hitches on a sling, as in this configuration, the angles are too wide for the sliding knot. The I directional (note how it is taut by use of the clove hitch) means the belayer can pull any which way and still be secure. And of course, she's run the belay rope through a directional at J.

It is very improbable that you would ever have to construct such an involved anchor at a popular sport climbing area. Bolts would have been sunk long ago. However, rigging such complicated anchors is required on most adventure climbs.

CON: We can pick apart any anchoring system, but this one is about as fundamentally sound as you can get, given the placements.

#32

ANCHOR #32: Two wired tapers (A and B), an alien SLCD (C), and a SLCD (D). A and C are connected with clove hitches tied into a sling (E). B and D are also connected with clove hitches tied into a sling (F). The E and F slings are tied together to form the anchor point for the lead rope (H). G is a directional for belaying.

PRO: This system, though confounding to observe, is really quite simple. The clove hitched slings maintain optimum direction of pull on the nuts, and by combining the two triangular components (F and E) at H, the entire system is under just enough tension to keep the placements well set. This is good security with minimum gear—four placements, four biners, two slings.

CON: Though a multi-directional anchor, strictly speaking it is not truly equalized. If the belayer should shift to his right, the D placement would take the brunt of his weight. And vice versa. Also, because the angle of the slings (the angle of the inside of the triangle formed by the slings) is so wide, the forces placed upon them is considerably higher than if the angles were narrower. As we've seen, as the angle of the sling approaches 60 degrees, the load at point A and D will increase to over 100% of the force applied at the tie-in point. Remember the rule: whenever possible, keep the widest angle less than 60 degrees, so loads are not multiplied on the outer two ends of the triangle. (At approximately 20 degrees the load would be equally divided at 50%.)

For direct in-line forces, this anchor is satisfactory. Even though the widest angle on the Spectra sling appears to be about 110 degrees, because the load is also absorbed by anchors B and C, the forces are never dangerously increased.

COMMENTARY: Though simplicity itself, this system requires savvy to rig, and a master's touch with the clove hitch to snug everything up. Such tricky constructions require practice to perfect. Leaving even the slightest bit of slack in either of the triangular sling setups (F and E) would result in an uneven distribution of forces on the placements. Whenever various components/placements of an anchor are tied off either directly by the lead rope, or with slings (like Anchor #32), a little tension in the system is advisable not only to equally distribute potential forces, but to keep the placements in their optimum position. When SLCDs are loosely connected and get jostled around as a belayer weights and unweights the anchor, said SLCDs can "walk." To accomplish a snug system normally requires that the belayer pull things tight before tying the knot (here, at H) at the anchor point. A haphazard, loose knot at H compromises the entire system. It cannot be overstated: whenever a sling (or any construct) connects two or more placements in a triangular configuration—the wider the angle, the more multiplication of forces on the placements. Whenever possible, rig the system with narrow angles (less than 60 degrees).

ANCHOR #33: Two wires (A and B), connected via a sling with the sliding knot, a wire (D) and a TCU (E) connected with a sling (F), two SLCDs (G and H) clipped off mutually at I, all three groupings are tied off with a cordelette (J).

PRO: All placements are sound. All three strands/branches of the cordelette are connected to separate anchor systems— good for multi-directionality. The cordelette connects the system in a clean, straightforward manner. Nice narrow angles on the C and J combinations. And the whole system is snug.

CON: Two concerns. The F sling is simply looped through the biners on placements D and E. Since the angles are somewhat wide to begin with, this pulley-type rigging multiplies the forces even more. Sometimes the pulley rig is necessary, even critical, to the security of the individual, especially when direct force is needed to keep the nuts well set. Because this is not a problem, it may be better to clove hitch the F sling into the D and E nuts. As we've discussed, when two placements are joined together at a mutual point— either with one biner or, in the case of I, with two biners—if one extends a fraction of an inch farther from the rock than the other, you don't get an equalized load. Better to rig the sliding knot, like C. Again, this anchor is not multi-directionally equalized, an impossibility with the cordelette.

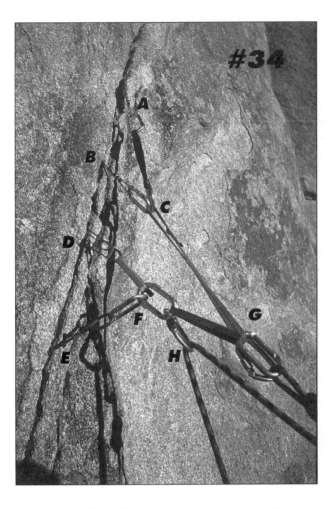

ANCHOR #34: Two wired tapers (A and B) mutually clipped off at C; a small SLCD (D) and an Alien SLCD (E) clipped off at F. A sling rigged with the sliding knot (G) connects the A–B, D–E placements. The belay rope runs through a directional at H.

PRO: The individual placements are good. The system satisfies all SRENE requirements but one crucial one: there is no redundancy at H.

CON: Not to abuse the point, but mutually clipping off two nuts at one point (F and C) rarely distributes the forces equally on the respective placements. For my taste, this system is rigged backward. Better to connect the placements with clove hitches (in a sling) or with a sliding knot (also on a sling), and tie the belay rope into these. The belay directional (H) is placing a 2X force on D.

ANCHOR #35: A cordelette tied with two branches. The A branch is clipped to two hexes (C and D), set in opposition; the B branch is clipped off to a sling (G) that is clove-hitched to a SLCD (F), and a hex (E) set in opposition.

PRO: A strong, multi-directional anchor featuring four bombproof nuts. Note how the G sling is clove hitched to the F and E placements to keep them taut against each other.

CON: This rigging is too complex given that the individual placements are so sound. It appears that a sharp downward load would place the bulk of the force on F, possibly resulting in slack enough to allow D to fall out.

COMMENTARY: There is nothing "wrong" with any element in this matrix, but the rigging is too elaborate. As a general rule, the better the nuts, the simpler the rigging. Gaudy, confusing rigging is typically called on only when the individual placements are less than ideal.

ANCHOR #36: A simplified, improved version of Anchor #35, featuring a bowline-on-a-bight (A) clipped to a hex (B) and a SLCD (C). The directional hex (E) is clove hitched (D) taut against the upper B and C placements.

PRO: Clean, simple rigging that illustrates the utility of the bowline-on-a-bight in equalizing two placements (here, the top hex and the SLCD). It is important to note how the oppositional E hex is clove hitched taut against the upper, weight-bearing placements. This removes any undesirable play in the system, and keeps things snug.

CON: Though each anchor must be assembled individually, when you have such bombproof placements as these, you can often avoid rococo rigging and simply anchor off with the climbing rope. Anchoring off directly to the placements with the climbing rope—as opposed to rigging slings on the placements—is only done when the climbing team is swinging leads. If one person is leading all the pitches, this method is impractical. The second can change over with his own set of biners (one on each piece), and a similar knot on his end of the rope, but this is a lot of extra fiddling in any event. Better to go with the cordelette, or some other system that the second is not required to re-build—or in some way re-rig—when he gains the belay. The other drawback, already mentioned, is that when tying the rope straight into anchor, more rope is used. This is rarely a problem, as precious few pitches use all one hundred and sixty five feet of the lead rope. But if you need that extra foot or two of rope, and don't have it, you're pretty much stuck, and have to pull all kinds of shenanigans while the belayer rerigs the anchor with slings to get you the needed few feet. A last drawback is the complicated reslinging necessary in order to escape. (Ref. Rules of Thumb #5.)

ANCHOR #37: Same setup as Anchor #36, but now the belay rope has been rigged as a directional off top hex (A).

PRO: Most everything.

CON: Aside from the considerations mentioned in Anchor #36 (swinging leads and using extra rope to rig the anchor), the only glaring fault is that the directional at A is clipped through one hex, rather than through the multi-directional anchor point.

A common mistake climbers make is to learn a bag of rigging tricks, then look for opportunities to employ them, even when they're inappropriate. Providing that the anchor is solid, simple is almost always better. For instance, if you're rigging a belay consisting of four burly hexes, there's no need to equalize two sets of two nuts, then in turn equalize the two pairs with a cordelette, or whatever. Just because a more involved system is stronger does not make the system superior to a easier, simpler setup. Often it makes it worse, as it uses unnecessary gear and takes too long to rig and break down. A bombproof anchor means it's good enough to withstand the greatest forces that a climbing team can place on it, which virtually never exceeds 2,500 lbs. That means a belay that can withstand 10,000 lbs. of force is no better than a system that can withstand 4,000 lbs. In short, avoid overrigging. Keep things simple and direct. A complicated anchor is always hard to evaluate. (Ref. Rules of Thumb #7.)

COMMENTARY: The matter of anchor overkill brings to light the differences in philosophies that given climbers have and swear by. For instance, Yosemite guide Dave Bengston told me I was ridiculous to say that a belay that can hold 10,000 pounds is no better than one that can hold 4,000 pounds. He cited engineering standards, which are set by a safety factor that is 4X the maximum working load. The point is well taken, and should be heeded particularly by those who are not accustomed to setting protection and cannot accurately gauge how good, or bad, their placements are. When in doubt, always add more, no matter how involved. However, once you are certain of your ability to evaluate the strength of your placements, strive to keep the system as simple and clean as possible.

The following examples depict several methods of anchoring off to solid placements. Often it is unnecessary to use slings in arranging such a belay, for you can simply tie the placements off with the climbing rope— a standard maneuver.

ANCHOR #38: Three SLCDs (A, B and C). The top (A) SLCD is tied off with an overhand knot (D), the lower two SLCDs are tied off with clove hitches (E and F).

PRO: Owing to the dark crack, you can't see how bomber all three SLCDs are. And as we've said over and over, a sound anchor begins with sound placements. The rigging method— overhand (or better yet, figure eight) knot on top, followed by clove hitches below—is a standard, quick and efficient way to connect bomber placements in a vertical crack.

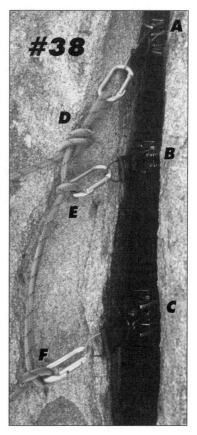

CON: Throughout the '70s and into the '80s, this was the usual way to connect various anchor components in a vertical crack. Naturally enough, this construction came out of Yosemite, where vertical cracks are the rule. This rig does, however, illustrate the drawbacks with the old system. First, the rope is too loose between the placements. In-line anchoring is only effective in equalizing the load if the entire system is taut— meaning when weight is applied on the rope beneath the F placement, the force is absorbed by A and B as well as F. Secondly, this direct-line setup is only effective when the direction of pull is straight down. Here, the SLCDs are all set for a slightly outward pull, evidenced by the attitude of the stems, which point more outward than downward. As is, if this rig were shockloaded with a downward jolt, the SLCDs would all pivot in line with the load. Not good. To shore up this anchor you'd realign the SLCDs, and lose the slack in the rope between placements. Of course, without a directional for upward pull, this system is good only for downward forces. (Ref. Rules of Thumb #5.)

COMMENTARY: This in-line setup is the simplest way to rig bomber nuts in a vertical crack. But again, effectiveness depends on the placements being set in the direction of anticipated loading, and that the rigging be taut as a bowstring. Mastery of the clove hitch is essential in attaining a degree of equalization (and equalization is always imperfect when tying anchors off with the climbing rope). Also, this setup should be rigged so the rope coming from the belayer's harness goes directly to the lowest placement (here, F). If the belayer is tied straight off to D, and D should fail, everything shockloads onto B. Though this is a viable rigging construct when properly arranged (taut), it has liabilities, particularly when the direction of pull is not consistent with the attitude of the crack and the placements therein.

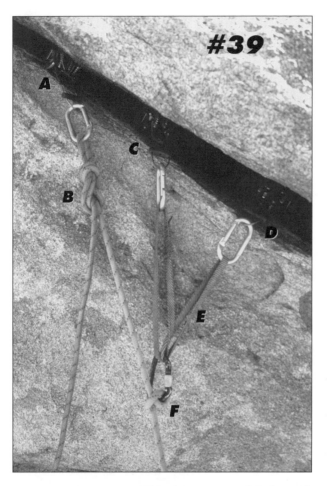

ANCHOR #39: Three SLCDs (A, C and D). Top placement (A) is tied off with a figure eight (B). Placements C and D are equalized with a sliding knot (E) and tied off with a clove hitch (F).

PRO: A strong, straightforward setup that, by virtue of the sliding knot (E), allows for some latitude in the direction of pull. That is, force can be applied onto the rope below F from any number of directions, and F will adjust itself accordingly. Simple and effective.

CON: Without a directional for upward pull, this is not a fully multi-directional anchor. The other hazard is the same that you always face when using the sliding knot: failure of either the C or D nut will put so much slack into the system that A will have to absorb the whole load (a pull to the right would also cause this). Here, this is an acceptable risk because both the C and D nuts are bomber, and the angle described by the E sling is minimal. The important point is to understand the potential consequences of the sliding knot, and avoid using it whenever the placements are less than ideal. When the placements are hale, as they are here, the sliding knot is a valuable tool. (Ref. Rules of Thumb #2.)

ANCHOR #40: A small stopper (A), and two TCUs (B and C). The C placement is a directional. Clove hitches at D, E and F connect the three placements.

PRO: All three placements are A1, and the rigging is snug and fast to install.

CON: The main problem is one that you cannot see, though it's suggested by the tautness of the rope at G—namely, that the belayer is tied directly off to D. If the stopper (A) blows, the belayer falls twice the distance between D and E (roughly three feet) and shockloads onto a measly TCU. In short, this system should be rigged bottom to top, with the rope from the belayer's harness going directly into the F directional. Also, the E clove hitch needs readjusting so the sling coming off the TCU (B) is under direct pressure. There's slack in it now, so it bears none of the load. Again, cinching the clove hitch in exactly the right position is crucial to make the knot work for you, not against you.

Finally, I never like belaying off only three small placements, no matter how well set they are. With this setup you have only six dinky cams and a taper the size of a quarter contacting the rock. Not enough for my money. (Ref. Rules of Thumb #5.)

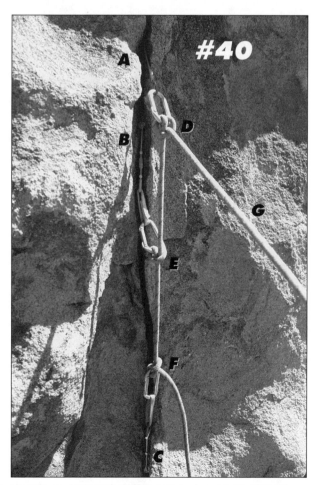

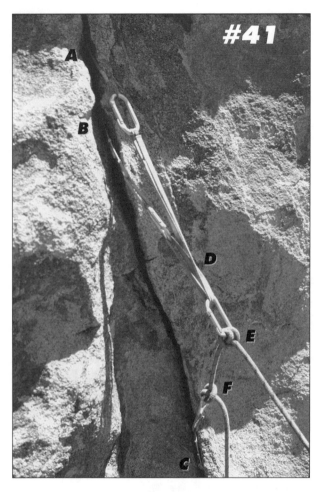

ANCHOR #41: A revision of Anchor #40 (page 67). A sliding knot (D) has been used to connect/equalize the A and B nuts.

PRO: A and B are the primary, load bearing nuts in this system, and being small, it's probably good to equalize them.

CON: You've got a calamity if A or B fails, so as mentioned, if either nut is less than bombproof, you should avoid the sliding knot. And that's the Catch-22: If the nuts are bomber, there's no need to equalize them. Either way, there is no redundancy at D. It is also rather unnerving and ill-advised to have the whole shooting match tied off to one biner at E. Better to double them, or at least a locking biner.

COMMENTARY: This scenario points up a riddle that we all occasionally face when constructing anchors—that for every reason there is to rig things one way, there are equal reasons to rig it differently. Here, you don't want to hang your hide off a puny wire and a TCU without them being equalized, but if you equalize them and one rips, you're well nigh buggered. Twenty-five years ago the solution was elementary: slam in a couple three pegs and call it good. The modern solution is to go with the cordelette, or to rig separate slings to A and B.

ANCHOR #42: Two SLCDs (A and B) and a directional hex (C). The top (A) SLCD is secured with a figure eight; clove hitches (E and F) secure the lower placements (B and C).

PRO: A and C are all excellent placements. There is no slack in the system, and the C hex affords a modicum of directionality.

CON: As with #40, the belayer is tied straight into D, meaning that if the anchor is impacted, the force will be transmitted along G and the A SLCD will have to weather the storm. If it blows, you've got major shockloading onto a marginal SLCD jammed in the back of a flare—a skull and crossbones scenario if ever there was one. This setup needs to be rerigged from the bottom up. As is, you're essentially belaying off one nut (A); and no matter how bomber A is,

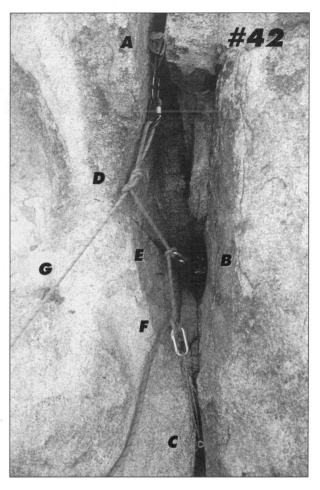

one nut is never enough for an anchor. Also, as is there's no sound place to run a directional to belay through.

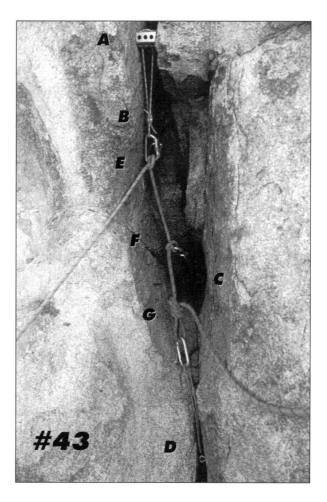

ANCHOR #43: A hex (A), two SLCDs (B and C), and a directional hex (D). One clove hitch (E) secures both the A and B placements, and the C placement is secured with another clove hitch (F). The directional hex (D) is secured with an overhand knot (G).

PRO: An improvement on Anchor #42 because two placements (A and B), rather than one, are positioned to absorb immediate loading.

CON: Again, like Anchor #42, this system is rigged upside down, because the belayer is tied directly into the A and B nuts (at E). Since these placements will absorb all loading, the D hex is superfluous—F is all the directional that is needed. However, this is far from a disastrous setup because the A and B placements are both rock solid and adequately equalized at E. Nonetheless, if the belayer was tied directly to D, followed by taut rigging up the line of placements, this setup would be stronger still.

ANCHOR #44: Two SLCDs (A and B) equalized by a sliding knot (the D sling) and secured with a clove hitch (E). A directional SLCD (C) is secured by a figure eight (F).

PRO: The placements are bomber, the rigging is tight and the system is clean and fast to install and remove.

CON: Two potential hazards: As always with the sliding knot (D), if either A or B fails, you'll get shockloading on the remaining placement. Second, because C is a directional, and is not weight bearing, you're essentially belaying off two placements (A and B) and essentially one sling—which means there is no redundancy. I would double-up the A and B grouping with a second grouping in the crack just left, and knit them into the system with another sliding knot. (Ref. Rules of Thumb #5.)

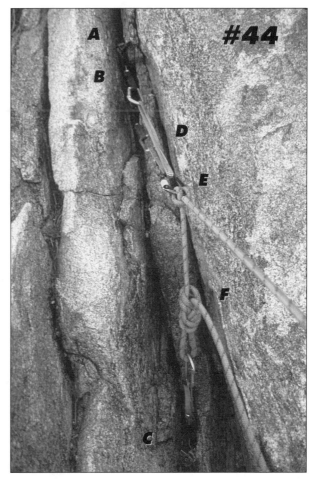

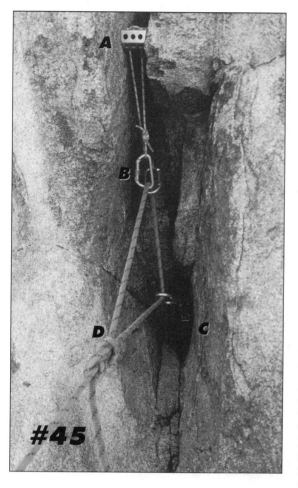

#45

ANCHOR #45: A hex (A), an unseen SLCD deep in the crack (B), and a directional SLCD (C), also deep in the dark crack. All three placements are connected with a figure eight-on-a-bight tied into the lead rope (D).

PRO: All placements are A1. The setup takes mere seconds to set up and remove.

CON: I always like to belay off four, rather than three placements, no matter how sound they are. Owing to the location of the placements, and their security, this is one of the rare instances where tying off all the components with one knot actually works. If these placements were anything less than A1, and if they were positioned differently (particularly if the B SLCD was lower), this setup would not adequately equalize the whole works.

COMMENTARY: As a rule of thumb, whenever you connect all the components of the anchor with one knot, once done, weight the system slightly (lean back on the anchor) and see how things look. Feel the slings/cord coming off each placement. Are they all taut? Is the direction of pull in keeping with the alignment of the placements? If you move about and place oblique force on the system, does the anchor remain equalized, or does one placement take most of the load? All of these things have to check out for this very simple system to work. Experience and a feel for subtleties will tell you when this kind of rig is acceptable, and when it is not.

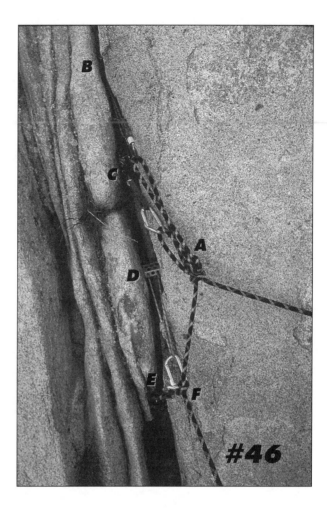

ANCHOR #46: A bowline-on-a-bight (A) clipped off to a hex (B) and an SLCD (C). A directional is accomplished via a hex (D) and an SLCD (E) clipped off together with a clove hitch (F).

PRO: All placements are solid. Good use of the bowline on-a-bight to equalize the B and C placements. The anchor is compact, tight and uses little gear.

CON: The D hex is bomber for downward forces, but the way the anchor is rigged, downward forces will never be applied to D unless B and C fail and the belayer shockloads onto D. As is, D accomplishes nothing; and as an oppositional, F is sketchy as it is set for an outward, not an upward, pull. Better to slot another nut at F that could withstand direct upward force, and clove-hitch it off taut to the bowline on-a-bight (A) for a snug, compact multi-directional anchor.

Flatirons, Boulder, CO
Photo: Beth Wald

Big Wall Anchors

One of the difficulties in studying big walls anchors is in photographing them. Or trying to. On a genuine big wall, so much equipment (the bulk of which has little to do with the anchor) is on hand, and the climbers are so close to the wall that getting a clear shot of the anchor is almost impossible. We can replicate systems near the ground, but they are not true representations of what you'll likely find on a wall.

The business of anchoring on big walls is a special study taken up in detail in *Big Walls!*, also in the *How To Rock Climb* series.

But understand this much: big wall mean big loads, which means equalization is all the more important; big wall anchors are complicated, requiring more time to rig, evaluate and to make sure things are as they should be.

Though by no means definitive, the following examples show several of the likely anchoring scenarios and setups that walls climbers face.

ANCHOR #47: Two-bolt belay equalized with cordelette. Black rope goes to climber through directional.

PRO: Though somewhat hard to make out, fixed slings, rather than the cordelette, form a triangle through the bolts. The cordelette forms a wishbone configuration, with the two upper prongs clipped off separately (at points A and B) into locking carabiners. Aside from the Atomic Rig (explained on page 18), this is the simplest, cleanest and fastest way to rig any two-bolt belay. Running the belay rope (C) through the A bolt increases the force times two, though here, where a climber is moving up to the belay, the increased forces are of no consequence; and in the event of a fall, it is much more comfortable for a ⅜″ bolt, rather than your waist, to absorb the load. Nevertheless, it's always best to run the directional through the equalized anchor point, rather than through one piece of pro.

CON: This is an optimum setup for in-line (straight up and down) forces. But since the cordelette is not a multi-directional system, a sideways force would load one bolt more than the other. (Ref. Rules of Thumb #4.)

COMMENTARY: There are basically two knocks against the cordelette: first, you must carry it. In practice, a few ounces of thin cordage (when doubled or tripled and worn over the shoulder like a sling) is such a trifling item that you won't get ten feet up a pitch and before forgetting that you even have the cordelette with you. Though useful on sport routes, the cordelette comes into it's own on adventure climbs, or wherever involved belays must be built quickly and easily. The second knock is that the cordelette (as featured in the photo) is not a multi-directional system. This is not inherently dangerous, particularly if significant sideways forces will never be applied—as is the case with many routes, which follow a more or less direct line. On paper, a multi-directional anchor is sturdier system, but the merits of any belay are judged by how effectively said belay safeguards against the forces that will be encountered. And for in-line face climbs, which climb directly up to a belay, and proceed directly off of it, the system featured in the photo is satisfactory.

ANCHOR #48: Belayer's eye view of three bolt hanging belay, haulbag (D) on right-hand bolt (A); directional on lower left bolt (C); cordelette used to equalize all three bolts.

PRO: Though impossible to discern, the top bolt (B) is an old ¼″ Rawl, and bolts A and C are ⅜″ threaded Rawl bolts. The cordelette has provided a handy solution to reducing the chance of shockloading on the A and C bolts—if B should fail. The tie-off features twin biners, gates opposed, and the haulbag (D) is off to the side and somewhat out of the way.

CON: The biggest problem here is that this system is rigged to haul the bag off one bolt. Most of the force that the anchor will encounter (save a Factor Two lead fall directly onto the belay) will come from hauling the bag. With big bags—which invariably get stuck at times and must be winched up with brute force—the anchor must bear a king-sized load. Much safer to rig a second cordelette of the B and C bolts for hauling purposes.

The other problem is one of inconvenience, not safety. There is no logic to the position of the bolts, so everything must be rigged so the whole shebang is essentially on top of itself—a standard headache on walls, where hanging belays must be built in vertical cracks. Ideally, the bolts would be spread out a little more. Otherwise, it's going to get cramped once the belayer gets to the belay station.

COMMENTARY: This anchor, from a Grade V wall in the High Sierra's, is an unusual and potentially confusing setup because on the majority of walls, the second climber usually jumars to follow/clean the pitch. So why is the lead rope rigged with a directional at C to belay the second climber up to the belay? Because this particular wall is mostly free climbing, and the second climber on the rope wanted the pleasure of following the pitch free, rather than jumaring it. (Whatever the reason, the directional should be running through the equalized anchor point.) This takes far more time, as the leader must first haul the bag before they can belay. But everyone's not out to set speed records.

ANCHOR #49: Same anchor as #40, but stripped down to clearly show the elements.

PRO: The improvement here is that the B cordelette is now rigged so one can haul off of it, rather than off the C bolt, as before.

Normally you would want to haul off the main equalized anchor point (A), but here the bag was light, and two bolts were thought to be sufficient for hauling off.

CON: This system is a good example of making the best of a less than ideal belay station (because of the bolts in less-than-perfect rock). Still, you can easily see the slack in the left-hand branch of the cordelette, connected to the C bolt. As mentioned, any equalizing system depends on the rigging being somewhat taut, with no play in the lines whatsoever. Direct force will remove most of the play, but in this instance, the snugger branches of the cordelette will absorb the bulk of the load. This is easily remedied by making sure the individual strands of the cordelette are taut when you tie the figure eight knot at A.

Photo: Bob Gaines

ANCHOR #50: Three bolts (A, B, and C), equalized by a cordelette (D). A second cordelette (E) is rigged between the A and B bolts. The leader is hauling the bag at F, the pulley connected to the A bolt, which is backed up by a sling (G) in case the A bolt should fail.

COMMENTARY: As usual with anchors on big walls, overlapping systems involve so much gear that understanding precisely what is going on can confound a man— or woman. Let's clarify this system, then critique it afterward.

This anchor system was assembled like this: the leader nails up to this three-bolt (A, B and C) hanging belay, clips off a bolt and ties in. Seeing the three bolts and nothing else, the leader decides to equalize the bolts with a cordelette (D), then he ties the lead rope (H) off at the cordelette, and also at B and C. Because you always want to haul the bag off to the side—and never off the middle bolt and cramp everything even worse—the leader decides to haul off the left-hand (A) bolt. He sets the pulley/hauling rig up off A, and backs this up by clipping a sling (G) off the A bolt into bolt B.

Deciding he does not want to hang two climbers and a 100 lb. haul bag all at one point, a second mini-cordelette has been rigged (E) to hang additional personnel and baggage, and to limit certain snags from having too many biners clipped into one point. (Better still would have been to rig the E cordelette off all three bolts. Equalize! Always equalize!)

Once you break the system down like this, you see that for all the biners, slings, pulleys and cordelettes, the entire rig is actually rather simple: a cordelette (D) equalizing the three bolts for the lead rope; a second cordelette (E) for additional anchoring purposes; and the hauling/pulley system at F. Again, what makes this appear complex is the overlapping systems, not the systems themselves.

PRO: Seeing that this hanging belay consists of three bolts in desert rock, the leader was wise to equalize them with the cordelette. The hauling system is rigged off to the side, and is backed up somewhat by the G sling. This entire setup is relatively clean and straightforward.

CON: One potential danger that cannot be helped: a previous party has retreated from this belay, and rather than leave a couple rappel slings through the bolts, they affixed lap links through the A and B bolts. Because these are old-style bolt hangers, the eye of the hangers are completely taken up with the lap links, so you can't clip into the hangers directly, but only the lap links. Lap links are not known to break. In fact they are stronger than carabiners. But you never want to add an unnecessary extra link in the system, no matter how strong that link is. But short of hauling along a hack saw, this cannot be helped.

So far as the rigging goes, the E cordelette was a good idea, insofar as it spreads the load between the A and B bolts for hauling purposes (which with all the heaving on a heavy bag puts considerable force on the anchors), but the bag is not being hauled off the equalized cordelette (E), rather straight off the lap link on the A bolt. True, the bolt is backed up with a sling (G), but that sling is clearly loose. Better to haul directly off the E cordelette, especially when hanging from bolts in soft desert rock. And as mentioned, the E cordelette should have been rigged to all three bolts.

ANCHOR #51: Three bolts (A, B and C), chained together and connected by a quicklink (D). A cordelette (E) equalizes the A and B bolts, and is connected at F with a Spectra sling (G) clipped off to a SLCD (H). The rope from the leader goes to the clove hitch on the quicklink (I), and is backed up via a figure eight knot (J) at the top bolt (B). The follower choose to follow the pitch free, so the climbing rope was clipped through a direction at K. L is a Gri-Gri, set for hauling.

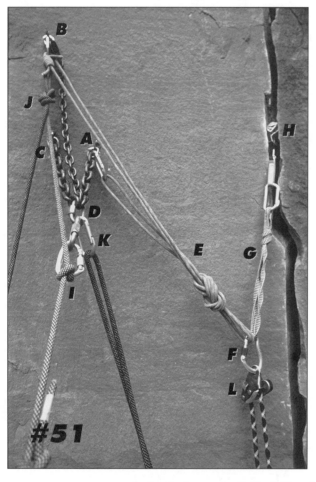

COMMENTARY: As this was a one-day ascent, the haul bag was actually a day pack (10 lbs. max). The leader has set up a hauling anchor using a cordelette (E) on the top two anchor bolts (A and B), joined with a Spectra sling (G) coming off a bomber SLCD (H) in the crack. This distributes the load for hauling, but more importantly here (as the bag weighs so little), it spreads out the anchor to accommodate two climbers and a bag at the sling belay.

The potential dangers of this belay, and ones like it, is the chain. Unlike webbing, you cannot adjust a chain to the tiny tolerances needed to equalize a belay anchor. Here, the chain coming off the B bolt is loose, so it absorbs none of the force. It is merely a backup. Since the chains coming off the A and C bolts join at the quicklink (D), they are equalized, but only in a very limited direction of pull. Lateral loading places all the force on one or the other bolt. What to do?

If the bolts look solid, as these do, and the several chains are relatively taut when the anchor is weighted, and, if the chain itself looks in good condition as well as the laplinks and the quicklinks, most climbers go with the chain matrix and call it good. Any doubts, back it up. If the bolts look solid but the chain looks worked (is rusty, or loose, etc.), clip off the laplinks directly and rig a cordelette—and back that up if need be.

A last note: I've included this chain setup because ones like it are often found on certain big climbs. The normal reasons are three: 1) the lower half, say, of the route is all free and is popular to do as a route in itself; 2) the climb is a trade route, and with all trade routes, many more teams start the climb than finish it. Over time, fixed rappel stations (like #51) are installed to accommodate easy retreat; 3) because the route is on a spire or free-standing formation without an easy way off, the climbing route serves also as the descent, and fixed anchors are installed to that end. In each case, traffic—and usually a lot of it—has prompted the fixed rappel stations, so if the whole works was going to fail, it probably would have long before you got there. But not always. Some of these setups are tragedies waiting to happen. The rule of thumb: Never trust a fixed anchor outright, no matter how stout it appears. Corrosion and metal fatigue—some visible, and some not—are inevitable to chain setups. The components of such rigs—the laplinks, chain and quicklinks—were not made to climbing specs. These are construction/industrial tools. Good enough if in good shape, trouble if haggard. Check everything before trusting your life to it, and back it up if there are any doubts.

ANCHOR #52: A closer look at the bolt/chain components of Anchor #51.

Access: It's everybody's concern

the ACCESS FUND

THE ACCESS FUND, a national, non-profit climbers' organization, is working to keep you climbing. The Access Fund helps preserve access and protect the environment by providing funds for land acquisitions and climber support facilities, financing scientific studies, publishing educational materials promoting low-impact climbing, and providing start-up money, legal counsel and other resources to local climbers' coalitions.

Climbers can help preserve access by being responsible users of climbing areas. Here are some practical ways to support climbing:

- **COMMIT YOURSELF TO "LEAVING NO TRACE."** Pick up litter around campgrounds and the crags. Let your actions inspire others.

- **DISPOSE OF HUMAN WASTE PROPERLY.** Use toilets whenever possible. If none are available, choose a spot at least 50 meters from any water source. Dig a hole 6 inches (15 cm) deep, and bury your waste in it. *Always pack out toilet paper* in a "Zip-Lock"-type bag.

- **UTILIZE EXISTING TRAILS.** Avoid cutting switchbacks and trampling vegetation.

- **USE DISCRETION WHEN PLACING BOLTS AND OTHER "FIXED" PROTECTION.** Camouflage all anchors with rock-colored paint. Use chains for rappel stations, or leave rock-colored webbing.

- **RESPECT RESTRICTIONS THAT PROTECT NATURAL RESOURCES AND CULTURAL ARTIFACTS .** Appropriate restrictions can include prohibition of climbing around Indian rock art, pioneer inscriptions, and on certain formations during raptor nesting season. Power drills are illegal in wilderness areas. *Never chisel or sculpt holds in rock on public lands, unless it is expressly allowed* – no other practice so seriously threatens our sport.

- **PARK IN DESIGNATED AREAS,** not in undeveloped, vegetated areas. Carpool to the crags!

- **MAINTAIN A LOW PROFILE.** Other people have the same right to undisturbed enjoyment of natural areas as do you.

- **RESPECT PRIVATE PROPERTY.** Don't trespass in order to climb.

- **JOIN OR FORM A GROUP TO DEAL WITH ACCESS ISSUES IN YOUR AREA.** Consider clean-ups, trail building or maintenance, or other "goodwill" projects.

- **JOIN THE ACCESS FUND.** To become a member, *simply make a donation (tax-deductible) of any amount.* Only by working together can we preserve the diverse American climbing experience.

The Access Fund. Preserving America's diverse climbing resources.
The Access Fund • P.O. Box 17010 • Boulder, CO 80308